All in the Family
...Business

All in the
Family...
Business

*A Personal Memoir
and Corporate History*

George G. Raymond, Jr.

POSTERITY PRESS

Printed in the United States of America

ISBN 1-88-9274-12-7

Raymond, George G.
All in the family—business : a personal memoir and corporate history /
George G. Raymond, Jr.
p. cm.
ISBN 1-889274-12-7
1. Raymond Corp.—History. 2. Raymond, George G.
3. Materials handling equipment industry—United States—History.
4. Executives—United States—Biography.
I. Title.
HD9705.5.M374 R39 2001
338.7'6162186'092—dc21

POSTERITY PRESS, INC.
P.O. Box 71081
Chevy Chase, Maryland 20813

www.PosterityPress.com

To Robin:

My Partner

My Friend

My Wife

My Eternal Love

Contents

Foreword

D. BRUCE MERRIFIELD

ASSISTANT SECRETARY AND UNDERSECRETARY OF COMMERCE (1982–1989)
WALTER BLADSTROM PROFESSOR EMERITUS,
WHARTON BUSINESS SCHOOL, UNIVERSITY OF PENNSYLVANIA

Only about 5 percent of some 18 million incorporated businesses in the United States are publicly traded; they constitute just the tip of an iceberg. The great strength and diversity of the U.S. economy are largely invisible, because this huge and impressive economic engine—the strongest the world has ever known—is made up mostly of family owned and family controlled businesses.

"Family businesses" have generated most of the 80 million new jobs created since the 1982 recession, while the Fortune 1000 have lost about 40 million jobs over the same period through downsizing and restructuring. Moreover, on average, family owned and family controlled businesses have grown faster and more profitably than professionally managed businesses. (And what an array of enterprises fit the rubric of "family business." They range from the corner Mom & Pop shop to the Mars candy conglomerate and the Forbes publishing empire.)

It is in this context that this fascinating book describes one family company's three-generation history. During that progression, or evolution, the Raymond Corporation went from entrepreneurial start-up in the 1920s, through heroic survival in the Great Depression and World War II, to stabilization during the Post-War era, then growth and "reinvention," and finally to market leadership. This instructive account describes the painful generational transitions, and it is told with great honesty and self-deprecating humor by the second-generation CEO.

George Raymond, Jr. is the son of the risk-taking and micro-managing founder, George Sr., the entrepreneur of the "X" generation of the 1920s, the benevolent dictator who saw his company through the Great Depression and saved his small town. Conflict was inevitable between this style of autocratic management, and that of the following "builder" generation, e.g. George Jr. who developed a "team player, let's-make-things-better" participatory style of management. It touches the heart to realize the painful difficulties that must always be associated with letting go of something you have built, complicated by father-son conflicts of love and the need for forbearance. Deep anxieties (unfounded, it turns out, and rewarded with great success) are part and parcel of each transition.

Tremendous dedication by the second-generation CEO to transforming the company culture was largely responsible for success in the next stage of development. Sadly, the third transition was even more traumatic, and its pain was intensified by a mindless personal tragedy, the bolt-from-the-blue murder of a family member by an unrelated madman. That tragic coincidence notwithstanding, the "company first, family second" mindset, so common in a family business, was not compatible with that of the 1960s self-focused "Boomer Generation." The necessity then, to transition to professional management ended in a form of betrayal and then a cliff-hanging but remarkably successful strategy that saved the family's fortunes. Furthermore, though the family could not keep its firm grip on the company, this period of the Raymond history includes romantic serendipity, indeed a story of love and enduring marriage.

As personal odyssey and family memoir, *All in the Family... Business* is a gripping yarn and, well, it's hard to put down. Above and beyond that, moreover, from a management perspective this is a classic case history of a particular kind of business enterprise, the most common and popular economic entity in America. It should be read and studied by every owner of a family firm, every student of business management, every scholar and teacher in a business school. *All in the Family... Business* has that much to teach all of us.

All in the Family ...Business

Prologue

I have been a businessman all my adult life, for almost fifty years with a company my father resurrected in 1922 in the rural community of Greene, New York. Originally the company was called Lyon Iron Works, later Lyon-Raymond, and finally The Raymond Corporation, a name it still has today but under different ownership. In the beginning the company manufactured goods that any foundry might make in the early part of the century, almost anything a farmer or an individual might need, as long as it was made of iron and wood. In the intervening years, we began to manufacture the product that put us on the map, the Raymond narrow-aisle forklift truck, the battery-powered little workhorse that transformed the handling and storage of industrial materials and wholesale commercial goods. These eye-catching machines (thanks to our signature orange color) do the heavy lifting and carrying of all sorts of materials in industrial plants, office buildings, freight depots, and warehouses throughout the world.

By 1953, when my father named me president of the company, we were fast becoming a leader in the material-handling industry. When I retired as CEO in 1987, our product was the undisputed leader in electric narrow-aisle vehicles. Ten years later BT Enterprises, a Swedish firm, bought the company. BT did not raid Raymond. It was not a hostile takeover. I had no choice but to sell the company that my father had started and I had led all my adult life.

This is my story, the story of a man who ran a family business, and the difficulties and challenges he encountered in dealing with family, management, and shareholders, all inextricably linked. For most of my life I wore three hats; each one representing a different me but at the same time it was the same me: head of a typical nuclear family, president of a publicly held corporation, boss of a family business: father, executive, owner. That was my job as president and CEO of The Raymond Corporation: it was all in the family at first, and my professional life was devoted to that particular business. Thus this memoir, *All in the Family... Business.*

Many people have asked me why I wanted to write my autobiography. After all, I was not a celebrity, and Raymond wasn't a celebrity company like IBM or Ford. I wrote this book because my life and the life of The Raymond Corporation are in ways one story, a story of personal enterprise, struggle and achievement, as well as a story involving some unreached goals, one bolt-from-the-blue tragedy, some personal regret and even failure. Perhaps, in some way, my story will help others in family-run companies; they might learn from the mistakes I made and the successes I had—what to do and what not to do. But mostly I wanted to share the experiences of one who endeavored to follow and uphold the bedrock rules of honorable business: To be honest with all people, to act fairly in all dealings, to compete with vigor and decency, to build strong relationships at home and the office, to contribute to a better world.

I didn't always succeed, but I never quit trying.

1

Greene Youth

Nestled in the Chenango Valley, twenty miles north of Binghamton in the state's southern tier, Greene, New York, was a one-horse town when my father moved there from Brooklyn with his wife and two children in 1922. At the time, my sister was five and I was all of six months.

From the day he left Cornell University in 1911, my father nourished a dream of running and owning his own business. An efficiency engineer who had worked for various companies, including Taylor Instrument Company in Brooklyn, my dad frequently asked his sister's husband, Bob Barnard, who owned the best bakery in Binghamton, if he knew of any companies that might be for sale. Finally, my uncle mentioned Lyon Iron Works, located in Greene.

Founded in 1840 by Henry Lyon, the grandfather of the current owner-operator Walter Lyon, the company made a variety of products out of wood and metal, such as saws, wood-working machines, wheelbarrows, plows, harrows and many other types of farm equipment. Walter Lyon was my Uncle Bob's distant cousin, and my uncle promised my father an introduction to Walter Lyon, but nothing more. That was all the opening my father needed.

The company had been in the Lyon family for three generations and, as so often happens—indeed this might have been an omen—

each generation had less and less enthusiasm for the business that had provided family members with a comfortable living. In fact, Walter Lyon was noticeably unenthusiastic about his company. Which proves the old adage in family-owned businesses: first generation, yes; second generation, maybe; third generation, no. So my father, armed with the introduction from my uncle, drove to Greene, visited Walter Lyon, and talked him into selling him the company—lock, stock and barrel.

What made this feat so impressive was that my father had no money! For years I've said that he would have hocked everything he owned, including me, in order to buy Lyon Iron Works. Well, he didn't have to hock anything. The going price of $6,000 would be paid to Walter Lyon out of future profits. As soon as the ink was dry on the paper, my mother and father packed up our belongings in Brooklyn. I was only an infant, but I'm sure to my mother and sister moving to Greene was like moving to a foreign land.

My father had grown up in Owego, N.Y., only forty miles away, where his father, Frank Raymond, had painted buggies and made driver's whips. My grandfather was a man of few words. Once, sitting with him on the front porch of his house when I was seven or eight, I asked him where he'd lived as a kid. "Right here," he said. That pretty much ended the conversation, though in later years he told me, more than once, "I'm a damn Yankee, George, and proud of it!"

Obviously it was no great move for my father when he relocated in Greene; in many ways he was coming home. But my mother had grown up in Brooklyn, where her father, Joseph Austin Crombie, imported essences and oils used in the making of perfumes. He was a Scotsman, and his wife, Cora, was also Scottish. My father met their daughter, Madeleine, on a blind date, and it was love at first sight. She was a terrific dancer and taught ballroom dancing in Brooklyn. They were married in 1912. I remember my mother so clearly in those early days She had lovely dark hair and was taller than most women in Greene, at 5 foot 5. Once she left Brooklyn with my dad, she never taught dancing again—except to me.

From the start, Greene was my home, and from the start I loved it. Any boy who grows up in a small town has a feeling of oneness with his surroundings, even of ownership: he owns the streams, woods, bridges, the stores on Main Street, the shortcuts to the swimming hole and playing fields. Even the wind in his face and the clouds overhead. There was hardly a person I didn't know by the time I was eight, and nobody I didn't recognize. The town was one big family. While I loved my parents and they loved me, I was everyone's son.

I began going to the plant when I was all of eight years old; at the time we lived right across the street from my father's office. My dad once wrote in a company pamphlet, "George, Jr., became interested in material-handling equipment when nine years old. His playtime scooter, darting around the plant, was a Lyon Hydraulic Lift Truck." And well it was. That "scooter" was the best toy I ever had!

Of all the shops and sections that made up Lyon Iron Works in those early days, my favorite by far was the foundry with its distinctive smell of moist sand. A couple of the molders took a liking to me and showed me how to make molds, which, painstakingly, I then proceeded to do. What made that experience particularly memorable was that the molders actually used some of my molds to cast parts of real machines.

When I was ten Greene got its first traffic light. The refrain rang: "We're coming up in the world!" But in all the years I lived there after that memorable occasion, it never got another. It was the kind of town Norman Rockwell loved to capture, embodying as it did those values so often thought of as quintessentially American—industriousness, decency, love of family, individuality, political conservatism, and a strong sense of God. My father was raised a Presbyterian, my mother an Episcopalian; my mother's branch of Protestantism prevailed, and every Sunday as a family we went to the Zion Episcopal Church in Greene.

Like most of the boys growing up in Chenango County, I developed a fondness for hunting, fishing and trapping. One day my father paid 22 cents for a chance on a .22 caliber Remington pump in a raffle sponsored by our local barber, and he won. He gave me the rifle, my first, and every Sunday afternoon we'd have target practice in our backyard, which ran straight for two hundred yards to the Chenango River. After I'd learned the fundamentals, we'd tramp the neighboring hills and valleys, hunting rabbits, grouse, pheasants, and squirrels. My dad watched me carefully to make sure I observed all the safety precautions. The rule I remember best is the one that at first puzzled me. "Remember, George," he said, "it's always the 'unloaded' gun that kills someone."

My dad was authoritarian in bringing me up, but he was never mean; to this day I still follow the principles of fair play, honesty and respect that he so assiduously followed his entire life, in his business and personal relationships. But one thing my dad told me was not correct, and it took me a long time to realize it.

As an avid sportsman my father wanted a dog for hunting rabbits. A worker at the plant told him about a farmer out in the country whose beagle had had a litter of pups. So Dad took the family for a drive that weekend and we bought one of the puppies. As soon as we got home, I was given the job of taking it for its very first walk. It was a happy moment for me. I was excited and already loved the little fellow. Everyone commented on how cute he was as we walked along. When I got to Main Street, I stopped, but the puppy didn't. He scooted out into the road where he was hit and killed. I ran home in tears, screaming in anguish and guilt, thinking for sure my father would be furious. To my surprise he put a comforting arm around my shoulders. It was an accident; certainly I hadn't done it willfully, he said.

That very same day we drove out to buy a second puppy from the farmer. On the way home my father said he had one thing to tell me. I steeled myself for a lecture. With the new puppy I would have to be more responsible, would have to watch him more carefully, I thought. That wasn't it at all. What he said was, "George, men don't cry."

In my view I wasn't a man yet, but I took it to heart.

Not long afterward I was helping him, after my fashion, load the Model T for the bi-monthly trip to visit his parents, who lived in Owego. However it happened—maybe because I was small and in my father's way—he closed the car door on my thumb. I didn't just cry, I bawled my eyes out. He comforted me and walked me into the house where he bandaged my thumb. Then he said, "What did I tell you about crying? Men don't cry."

It took me fifty years to realize how narrow a statement that was. By then I had quite a few tears stored up within me, and I never held them back again if they ever wanted to spill out.

When I was old enough to go hunting by myself, I would often take Shorty, our beagle, with me. Lore has it that a cottontail will naturally run in a big circle when a dog jumps and chases it, wanting to get back to its hole, often passing close enough to the hunter so he can get a shot; but I swear Shorty had a lot to do with it, knowing instinctively where my father or I was standing. And what a voice! To hear him on a trail on a cold November morning was music to my ears.

One night after a delicious rabbit stew, prepared by my mother, my dad said, "We've George to thank for dinner tonight." I took it as great praise, and my chest swelled with pride.

I played all the sports that kids played in those days, especially football and basketball. My father had played semi-pro baseball in Owego in his late teens, and he taught me the game early on, but the truth is I wasn't very good at it. My strength was base-running, but you have to get on base to display that skill, and hitting was not my strong suit.

My aptitude for other sports more than made up for my lack of it in baseball, and sports, generally, played a big part in my young life.

While I may not have led the class, I was a good and certainly a determined student. Looking back, I can see that my interest in certain areas was definitely dampened, if not killed forever, by the harshness of a couple of my grade-school teachers. My third grade teacher, a severe woman with dry gray hair, told the class to draw an airplane. I struggled and struggled, and finally scratched out a set of wings, a propeller of sorts, and something that represented landing gear. She walked around the class looking at each student's work. She came down the aisle and picked up the drawing by the girl sitting across from me, then mine. Holding both aloft, she announced that the girl's was "the best" and George's was "the worst" in the class. That ended, right then and there, whatever interest in art I might have had.

Something similar happened the next year when another teacher asked me to stand up and sing the scale. I tried, but she shook her head and bellowed: "You don't know one note from the other!" If I had liked music, I didn't after that. Except for the most popular of Broadway musicals, I had hardly any interest in music throughout my adult life. Indeed, when I attended a performance of the Chicago Symphony when I was in my fifties, it was the first time I'd heard classical music played by a live orchestra.

What I enjoyed, and therefore pursued, were team sports and outdoor activities. I felt an affinity with the great out-of-doors. A country boy may not have the familiarity with famous composers and poets like the boy attending a New England prep school, but lines I would learn much later in life from a friend at Alfred University—lines penned by the poet William Wordsworth—made me realize that knowledge and wisdom aren't gained only in classrooms. "One impulse from a vernal wood/Can teach you more of man/Of moral evil and of good/Than all the sages can." I would not trade my childhood in Greene with any boy in America, and I do not believe any boy anywhere had a fuller education.

Among the outdoor activities I followed, while growing up, was trapping. I am not a defender of the activity today, and have no argument with those who would ban it for the pain and stress it causes wild animals. But as a boy I had a different view. Trapping required great patience and determination. Once traps were set, you had to visit them every day, regardless of conditions. Skinning and stretching the pelts took skill and a steady hand. Perhaps it was the future businessman in me, but I liked the fact that running a trapline put money in my pocket. Considering that we were in hard times in America, where every dollar counted, that was no small incentive.

I wasn't aware of my father's prominence in the community until I reached the sixth grade. By then the Great Depression had settled in and the entire town was feeling its effects. My teacher that year was Mrs. Schmoll; her husband, like so many other husbands in Greene, worked at my father's company. Almost every day during "quiet period"—a time for free reading or study or just thought—I went up to her desk to talk; but it wasn't only to talk. My real reason was to get out of studying! One time she told me how much the company, and the fact that my father was keeping it afloat despite the Depression, meant to the town of Greene. She described him as "the savior of the village."

"Savior" was a pretty powerful word, but I was proud she'd said it about my dad. He was a leader in the community, I knew that. He was always meeting with other businessmen to discuss topics of common interest. One of his friends was a man named Ed Weeks, who happened to be District Governor of Rotary, the international and quintessential service organization. My father asked Mr. Weeks if Greene could have a chapter of its own. Mr. Weeks said no, Greene was just too small. But my father kept after him and finally Ed Weeks gave in.

Perhaps if they went to Chicago to meet the founder and president of Rotary, Phil Harris, they could persuade Mr. Harris to see it my dad's way. I was too young to remember the occasion of my father's return, but I know he came home a happy man. The founder of Rotary had granted the little town of Greene, New York, a provisional charter. If its members followed the rules of Rotary for one year, then it could become a full-fledged member. History says they did, for in 1924 Greene became the first small town in America to have a Rotary charter.

As the Depression deepened, a cloud of fear and uncertainty hung in the air over Greene. There was no such thing as job security. If you had a job you were one of the lucky ones, and if you didn't, you were constantly looking for work. Companies with little or no business were soon companies with few or no employees. Just how my father held on was, as I look back on it now, an amazing accomplishment; but hold on he did. In 1932, things were so bad that Lyon Iron Works was down to two full-time employees—my father and Bill House, his right-hand man, and a secretary who worked halftime, Caroline Winchell.

It was right at this time, the very depths of the Great Depression, that my father came up with the idea that would revolutionize his company and launch it on its successful path through the rest of the century. Lyon Iron Works already had, as one of its products, the Hydraulic Grease Gun, used to force grease into the joints and bearings of heavy machinery. From this simple machine, my father got the idea for a hand-pulled hydraulic lift truck to pick up and move skids, the commonplace steel and wooden platforms on which goods were stacked for transfer and storage.

One such Hydraulic Lift Truck was produced, and then another and another; but these sales weren't enough to keep the company in the black. Buoyed nonetheless by the new truck and seeing its many applications, my father went around the countryside begging anyone who would listen to buy common stock in the company, mostly farmers who had somehow managed to store a few dollars in a glass jar somewhere. He convinced a sufficient number of people to invest in Lyon Iron Works—certainly a great feat of salesmanship!—and the company, with a staff of two men and a part-time woman, made it through the worst years.

As for life at our house, while we had it better than most families, it still wasn't much. We had to cut back during the hard times. Where pot roast had been frequent fare, we were lucky now to have it once a month. My mother made the best macaroni and cheese I've ever tasted, and to tell the truth I never grew tired of it. She was a great homemaker, and always a wonderfully supportive mother. Whenever I had to get my dad's permission on an issue involving his teenage son, I always went to my mom first. She would listen carefully, always with the mindset that her husband would give my request a thumbs down. She would then offer an enlightened opinion, which pretty much told me if my sales pitch would work on my dad.

My father took me with him on business trips and even to conferences when I was a boy. There were no other kids my age around, but I didn't care. I was having a terrific time and, as I suspect my father knew, I was learning. I can still recall some of the things he'd say on these trips, such as his comment that if you went into the plant superintendent's office and saw a cluttered desk, you could be sure that his plant would be cluttered and dirty as well. And if his desk was neat, the plant would be neat. In my later experience, the truth of those observations was almost always borne out. For the record, however, the floor of Lyon Iron Works was clean and orderly but my dad's desk—well, at best it was a C–. I should say that my desk, when I was old enough to have one, was never anything to write home about either.

At fourteen, working papers in hand, I got my first job at the company. It was in drafting, and I earned ten cents an hour. I'd taken mechanical drawing in school so, while I wasn't experienced, I wasn't a pure novice. My job was to copy machined parts that had changed over time and to bring the drawing of the part up to date. What I remember most clearly from that first job was that I worked in the second-floor wood shop where it was extremely hot in the summer, frequently 110 degrees or higher. I put a fan in the open window right next to my work table so that the breeze would, literally, blow my sweat away. Otherwise it would have dropped right on the paper I was drawing on.

By the time I got to high school in 1936, the grip of the Depression had eased somewhat. As I began my first year I was determined to enter the U.S. Naval Academy in Annapolis after graduation and become a navy officer. I even built my course of studies around that goal. However, just after the Christmas break, something happened that dramatically changed my life. Miss Cora Taft, who taught Greene High's mandatory Guidance Course spoke in class one day about "choices" in a very general way, but a bell went off in my head. Instead of Annapolis, I planned my high school studies for entrance to Cornell University, where my father had gone. I would study engineering as he had done. Young as I was, I realized what I really wanted to do was follow in his footsteps. Right then and there I switched my career goal from Annapolis to Cornell, from the navy to business: specifically my father's company.

That was my dream, but my first love in those days was football. Even though I weighed only 149 pounds, I was the starting center and captain of the team my senior year. What made this even more unusual was that we had a surplus of really big boys in our school that year, and our line averaged 235 pounds—with me in it! I don't think there was a college team in the area that could make that same claim.

I also was the back-up fullback. We used a double-wing formation, and ordinarily the quarterback would call the plays, but our coach, Johnny Grant, designated me the play-caller. Little did I realize at the time that this experience in leadership would benefit me for the rest of my life.

In addition to sports, I had a great time as a member of the Footlight Society, Greene High School's drama group, where I both acted and built scenery. I had little interest in music or art but I had always liked acting. Perhaps I had inherited a thespian talent from my mother, whose cousin and aunt were, respectively, Ruth Chatterton and "Mother Time," noted actresses of their day.

I played the lead in *The Valiant* and a well-known adaptation of *Huckleberry Finn*. In that play I did my own make-up as Huck's father, a down-at-the heels scoundrel, and no one—not classmates, not teachers, not even my own parents—knew who I was!

I also learned at this period in my life that I had good organizational skills. Shirley Edgerton, a senior at G.H.S. and good friend, was running for president of Student Council, and she chose me, a junior, to run her campaign. The front-runner was a popular boy and no one thought Shirley had a chance. But his popularity faltered against Shirley's organized campaign. It was a great come-from-behind victory.

At one point in the mid-1930s, when I was 15, my father sent me—alone—to visit a really big plant, the American Can Company in Hoboken, New Jersey. Lyon Iron Works made a square-platform, three-wheel truck for American Can, which workers used to transport sheets of tin plate from the presses to the lithograph machines. This three-wheel truck was, in fact, Lyon Iron Works' main product. Between American Can and Continental Can, orders would come to the Greene plant for 100 to 300 trucks at a clip. Seeing this huge operation at American Can gave me insight into the advantages, if not the requirement, of size in making a manufacturing company profitable. I was beginning to envision how I would do things at Lyon Iron Works when my day came.

Times started to improve, and gradually my father was able to hire back most of the workers he'd let go. He also began buying back the stock he'd had to sell, and aggressively drummed up new business. By 1938 the company was once again on a solid footing, and my father could see a much brighter future.

There was one man, besides my dad, who held a significant number of Lyon Iron Works shares, a Manhattan businessman by the name of Dumont, and in 1938 my father approached him with a proposition. They ought to have a buy-sell agreement, my dad said to Mr. Dumont, so that if one of them died the other would have the exclusive right to buy his shares in the company. Dumont thought this was a good idea and told my father to go back to Greene and draw up an agreement.

Dumont was quite a character; I know because my father took me along on that trip to Manhattan. Dumont belonged to the New York Athletic Club, and he talked my father into springing for a dinner party there for our biggest customer, American Can. I remember that Dumont even told my dad what the menu should be, and when my father asked what the difference was between wild rice and regular rice, Dumont's answer was, "Ten dollars a pound!"

Dumont had been married three times—something unheard of in Greene—and his current wife was a flashy blond many years his junior. In any event, the wisdom of my father's idea became evident much sooner than anyone had anticipated, for shortly after our return to Greene, but before my father had finished drafting the agreement, we got the news that Mr. Dumont had died! After waiting a decent interval, my father approached Mrs. Dumont, told her about the proposed buy-sell agreement, and offered to buy the stock from her which she had just inherited.

She agreed to sell, and came to Binghamton where she approved the details. My father's lawyer said it would take him two hours to finish drawing up the agreement, and she said she would wait. But then she realized that if she wanted to catch the 4 o'clock train back to New York, she would have to leave then and there; and so she did.

When the document was finished, my father signed it and sent it off. But instead of returning it signed and sealed, Mrs. Dumont held on to it. Knowing there were still small blocks of stock here and there around Greene, which he'd sold during the Depression, my dad saw that for his own protection he had better gather them all up. When he finally had all the certificates back in his possession, he owned 50.1 percent of Lyon Iron Works, a controlling interest.

What had happened in New York was that a former business associate of Mrs. Dumont's late husband, a man named Fink, had resurfaced. Both Mr. Dumont and Mr. Fink owned shares in Lyon Iron Works, but they'd had a falling out. In fact, Dumont had thrown Fink bodily out of his office. Nonetheless, Mrs. Dumont had joined forces with Mr. Fink and together they owned 49.9 percent. At the next annual meeting of the company they showed up together, and demanded full disclosure of all financial information, including my father's salary. If there was anything my father was secretive about, it was what he paid himself, which at the time was the healthy sum of $15,000 a year. During that period, most company presidents had similar views.

Despite his reticence to divulge his salary, he gave Mrs. Dumont and Mr. Fink the information "in strictest confidence." The next day, courtesy of Dumont and Fink, it appeared in our local paper.

Once that happened, it was war. They sued, as stockholders, alleging mismanagement, and it turned into a real donnybrook. By that time I was at Cornell but still working for the company during the summers, and Dumont-Fink et al. demanded copies of all my expense accounts, charging that I was using company money to visit my girl-friend, and future wife, who was attending Mount Holyoke College in Massachusetts. It was a gross contrivance on their part to gain local support and backfired in their faces.

The start of World War II was no deterrent to Fink and Dumont, and I was already in the army when the time for trial drew near. The judge, a man of reason, said, "Look, this is silly. Why don't you get together and compromise and save everybody time and trouble and money?"

That is what happened, and the case was settled out of court, with my father agreeing to buy the Dumont-Fink holdings. He now owned 100 percent of the company. Well, almost 100 percent. I owned one share. How I came to own that one share is another story; stay tuned. But once again Lyon Iron Works was "all in the family."

2

Company Boy
to Company Man

I n July of 1939 I started dating a girl by the name of Cynthia Spencer, whose family had been part of the Greene scene longer than the Raymonds. The Spencers' year-round address was White Plains, New York, where H. Dorsey Spencer, Cynthia's father, was a patent attorney. Greene was their summer residence.

Cynnie, as everyone called her, was eighteen, with lovely green eyes and brown hair. She wore it in a pageboy and I loved the way it framed her face. She was "petite," just over five feet, and had a wonderfully easy laugh. I especially liked the way she laughed at my jokes, which at times were pretty lame.

While it wasn't exactly love at first sight, eventually I was smitten. As were a couple of other guys in town. At the time of our first date, Cynnie was also going out with two friends of mine, both already in college. One worked nights at the Greene Hotel, the other during the day, and she'd see them, respectively, in the day and at night.

That Cynnie Spencer had other suitors brought out my competitive nature. I was determined to win her affections before I left for Cornell. She was a good tennis player, liked dancing, swimming and horseback riding, and we spent a lot of time together that summer. I even taught her how to play golf. I really don't know what happened to the other guys, but before I left for Cornell, and she for Mount

Holyoke, Cynnie and I were seeing only each other. Whether it was merely a "summer romance," however, I couldn't say.

Before I left Greene, my father took me aside; he had enough money to pay for the first two years of my college education—and might have enough for the final two. He said I could take the chance that this money would still be available, or I could get an on-campus job, which would all but guarantee me four full years at Cornell.

I thought about it a good deal. If my father had the money to send me to college now, certainly, with the company growing, he'd be able to pay for my junior and senior years as well. But I didn't like the feeling of having to depend on him, or anyone. I was always one to take matters into my own hands. I decided to look for a job.

As luck would have it, a job came looking for me. A recent Cornell grad from Greene, Nelson Bryant, called me, hoping to convince me to pre-pledge his fraternity. I declined his offer, wanting the chance to look around and make my own decision; but I jumped at the chance to ask him if he knew of any jobs. He said he'd worked at a sorority house, Kappa Alpha Theta, "the best sorority on the hill." I should go see Mrs. Case and tell her that Nelson Bryant had sent me.

I walked onto the Cornell campus just days after Germany invaded Poland. I heard the news but, basking in the atmosphere of a great college on the shores of beautiful Cayuga Lake, it didn't affect me. Germany and Poland? Whatever "war" they had going on wasn't my concern. My life, my goals, were here.

The course of study I'd be following was engineering. In the fall of 1939, Cornell had a student population of 6,000, and I was more than a little nervous about whether I'd be able to make the grade. It hardly helped that the very first Freshman Orientation speaker welcomed us to Cornell Engineering by saying, "Look at the person on your right, then at the one on your left. By the end of the first term, one of them won't be here." That was depressing, to say the least.

Nonetheless, always hopeful, and having a good bit of faith in myself, I embarked on a whirlwind schedule of classes and social activities.

I also went to see Mrs. Case at the sorority house. I was met at the front door by a Mrs. Bullock, who barked at me, "Who are you and what do you want?" But the bark of this robust black woman turned out to be far worse than her bite. When I told her Nelson Bryant had sent me, she softened immediately and sent me to Mrs. Case, the housemother at Kappa Alpha Theta.

Mrs. Case was a tall, attractive, well-kept woman. We had a good talk, and at the end of it she gave me the job. I joined a staff of two other waiters and two dishwashers. For some reason, Mrs. Bullock, who prepared the meals for the sisters of Theta, decided to give me cooking lessons, and when she saw I had a knack for the "culinary arts," she began teaching me everything she knew in earnest. It was a "course" at Cornell I never got credit for, but I was never sorry I had it. Mrs. Bullock's "Cooking 101" was to serve me well throughout my life.

Mrs. Case, who was a widow, had a male friend, who I soon found out was the Governor of Pennsylvania. When he visited I'd serve them their meals in her suite of rooms in the sorority. They were a handsome couple and I always enjoyed the talk we would have when I'd walk in with a tray.

When it came time to pledge a fraternity, I chose Phi Kappa Sigma; it had a great house on campus and the upperclassmen were a terrific bunch of guys. I was elected rushing chairman in my sophomore year, and the efforts of my team produced an outstanding pledge class. That same year I ran for house manager of Phi Kappa Sigma's dining room against an upperclassman; the winner would get his meals free, so it was definitely worth the try. During the period leading up to the election, my brothers definitely ate better than before, but I hadn't taken sufficiently into account something called "cost." As a result our food bills during that period were so high that we would have gone broke. Needless to say I didn't get the job. But I learned an important managerial lesson!

My job in the sorority kitchen turned out to have a fringe benefit. Mrs. Bullock had a gentleman friend, who was also a cook on campus. Every now and then they would stay out too late and consume too much alcohol, or as he called it, "firewater." One Friday at 5 A.M., she called and woke me up, saying she didn't feel so well. Would I hurry over to the sorority house and start making breakfast, and keep at it until it was time for my 9 o'clock class?

I put my cooking lessons to use that morning, to the full satisfaction and pleasure of the girls. Mrs. Bullock showed up a few minutes before 9:00, looking a little under the weather but most appreciative of the extra hours of sleep I'd enabled her to have. After class, I worked the lunch shift in the sorority, and when it was over, Mrs. Bullock asked, "George, got a date tonight?"

I didn't see how it fit into the equation but I told her that I did. She reached into her pocket and pulled out a set of keys. "Well," she said, "you can have my car until noon tomorrow. Just bring it back in one piece."

I could hardly believe it. She drove a Buick Roadmaster, arguably more "boat" than car, but it was one handsome automobile.

After that, whenever she and her boyfriend over-indulged, I took the early shift in the kitchen and was rewarded with Mrs. Bullock's keys. I didn't kid myself into thinking I was a big man on campus, but I sure felt like one behind the wheel of that Roadmaster.

As for my own social life, while I was surrounded by girls in the sorority, they were off limits. Sorority rules. If you worked in the Theta House, you couldn't date the sisters. I don't know how the authorities would have found out if you did, but I was sure it was done secretly here and there around campus. God knew the Kappa house had some really pretty girls in it and I was tempted.

Occasionally I went out with other girls but I kept thinking of Cynnie Spencer, whose heart I'd won at the end of the summer; at least I liked thinking I had. Hadn't she broken up with her other beaus? Perhaps that wasn't the same thing. But this much I was starting to think. Maybe it was Cynnie who'd won my heart.

One of the best times of the whole school year at Cornell, was House Party Weekend, which took place each spring. Hoping Cynnie was still interested in me, I invited her to come down from Mount Holyoke. She accepted, and I took it as a good sign, though I still wasn't sure. Quite possibly she wanted to come for the House Party Weekend, and I was merely the facilitator. But when the weekend finally ended, all the partying and sports events over, we both knew that our "summer romance" was more than a summer romance. This could be the real thing.

When Cynnie arrived for the same weekend the following year, I asked her if she would wear my fraternity pin. She accepted, and I pinned it on her cashmere sweater. We were now "engaged to be engaged." We kissed, and looking into her brimming green eyes and telling her that I loved her, I thought it was the happiest moment, thus far, in my life.

The Germany-Poland business hadn't passed as an isolated incident, and what was now going on overseas was everyone's concern. Cayuga Lake was a wonderful place to be, but smoke from the fighting in Europe and in the Far East was spreading around the world. In the summer of 1942 I was "prime" for the service. Largely for this reason, Cynnie and I decided to get married. The wedding party was a grand affair, held in the yard of the beautiful old barn the Spencers had converted to a comfortable home, three miles outside of Greene. It was a wonderful place for a reception, and all the members of both families had a splendid time. Cynnie and I were both twenty years old.

Because so many men had already been drafted, my father was having trouble hiring competent replacements in his company, especially for managerial posts. So that fall I took a leave of absence from Cornell to serve as his sales manager. I'd done a good job academically and the University said I could come back anytime.

I was happy to be working with my father again—he had recently changed the company's name from Lyon Iron Works to Lyon-Raymond—and he, in turn, was glad to have me back on board. On my twenty-first birthday, that November, he staged one of his characteristically dramatic gestures, as if to prove that point.

We were in New York City. I was there to help man our booth at the Power Show, a big event in the material-handling industry held each year in Madison Square Garden. On the night of my birthday, my father, mother and I went out to dinner. Over cocktails, he said to me, "You have a decision to make, George. As your birthday present you can have one hundred dollars cash, right now, or one share of Lyon-Raymond stock. I guess I don't have to tell you that a hundred dollars is worth a hundred dollars, and you couldn't sell this stock for a penny."

I didn't have to think about it for one second. "I'll take the stock." I loved the company and I wanted to be a part of it.

I not only took it, I had it framed under glass, then hung it on my office wall. Of all the different offices in the company I've had since that day, it's always the first personal touch that goes in.

The war effort in the United States was at full speed, and one step ahead of the draft I joined the Army Air Corps in February of 1943. At least that was my plan. The head of the local draft board, who happened to be a friend of my father's, alerted me that my number was very likely to come up the following month. If I waited until then, I would be included in his "quota." However, he told me I could still sign up for the Army Air Corps when I went to the induction booth at Fort Niagara.

When I got there I was met with a rude surprise—the induction booth wasn't there. Sorry, a gruff-talking sergeant informed me, we took it down last week. I asked him why. Pilots became officers upon completion of their training, he said, so the Air Corps was having no trouble filling its quota.

Thwarted and disillusioned, I entered the Army as a draftee and was assigned to an anti-aircraft unit in Fort Bliss, Texas, where I would be trained in the use of ninety millimeter anti-aircraft guns. But I wasn't giving up on the Air Corps. I was determined to be a pilot, and I continued pushing for a transfer.

The gun commander of my battery at Ft. Bliss was a buck sergeant who stood 6 foot 6 and had everyone scared half to death. He was mean, short-tempered, and tough as nails. We were in the field for exercises one day with three other batteries, each comprising four guns mounted on wheels, when a cloudburst caused all the gun carriages to sink into the sand past their hubs. Once we had freed our guns from the mire, the sergeant yelled for a "wheel puller." The axles were caked with sand and would have to be cleaned before we could move out, as the whole force had been ordered.

I was supposed to have the device in my kit, but for some reason it was missing. When I told this to the sergeant, he grabbed me by the front of my fatigues and lifted me off the ground. "Find the god-damn thing," he shouted into my face, "so we can get outta here. I wanna be first!"

More angry than intimidated, I yelled back, "So does everyone in the battery, Sergeant! This isn't how to do it!"

With an expression of surprise, if not shock, he released his grip. A concerted effort turned up the wheel puller, and soon we were "outta there," first in the column of big guns. From then on when he spoke to me, I liked thinking it was with a certain respect.

My persistence in joining the air wing appeared to be paying off. Shortly before I was to leave Fort Bliss, I took a battery of tests and had a number of interviews, and was told that my transfer to the Air Corps would come through after we arrived in California, our next post. This news did not endear me to the brass in my AA unit; they didn't want anyone leaving their ranks, especially someone who had displayed technical know-how and proficiency. By then I had earned the three stripes of a technical sergeant.

I was in the middle of the Mojave Desert, on exercises, when my papers came through, ordering me to report to the U.S. Army Air Force the next day at Ontario Air Base, 25 miles away. I went to the top sergeant of the company, a squat man with bull-like eyes, and asked him what I thought was a fair question. "How do I get there?"

"You've got two legs," he snarled. "Walk!"

"Whatever you say, Sergeant."

"There's a bus at 1800 hours. *Maybe* you'll be on it."

It was just after four in the afternoon, and he let me twist in the wind until 5:55 before okaying my ride.

From Ontario Air Base, my new buddies and I were shipped to the University of North Dakota, by way of Denver, where we were to receive six weeks of training. In the fifth week, at which point I already had ten hours of flight time, we were told we were being sent to Santa Ana, California, where we were to be measured for our uniforms as Air Corps Cadets, and where we would immediately begin our pre-flight training.

To say I was excited is a huge understatement; all of us were gung ho when we arrived in Santa Ana. Then it all came crashing down. The 15,000 of us in the program were herded into large theaters and read a telegram from Hap Arnold, the Air Corps' commanding general. It informed us that the Corps had too many flying officers at present; we were being transferred back to the ground forces, namely, the mud-slogging infantry I'd just left! All of us were fit to be tied. When my disappointment finally subsided, I found myself on the

Hunter-Liggett military reservation halfway between Los Angeles and San Francisco.

It was anything but exciting duty; a lot of make-work details. One time a duo of older soldiers, who'd recently been busted to pfc, were the only men in a group under my supervision who were actually doing what they were supposed to do: pick up trash around the reservation. I told the older soldiers to knock off, then ordered the slackers to finish the job, on the double! They groused and kicked but did as told. Later, one of the older soldiers took me aside. "Me and Wilson didn't think you had it in you," he said. "You showed us something, sergeant."

I was learning stuff I'd never learned in college.

In October, 1944, while at Camp Butner, North Carolina, I received a phone call that sent me hurrying to Cynnie's side in White Plains. Our first child, just born, had a birth defect, spina bifida, the incomplete closure of the bony encasement of the spine. I contacted a surgeon at Cornell Hospital in New York City who said he could operate, but added, "Your daughter's chances of surviving are slim. She'll always be paralyzed. I think you should just let nature take its course."

Painfully we followed his advice, and a week later the baby died. It was devastating for both of us, but Cynnie took it especially hard. I never thought she'd stop crying. She came back to Camp Butner with me and we were closer than we'd ever been. Our shared loss brought us together and made us fully understand the meaning of marriage. To stand by one another, in sickness and in health, for better or for worse. I kept telling Cynnie that we'd have other children. She wanted to believe we would, but it took a long time for the sadness to go from her eyes.

Our stay at Camp Butner lasted two months. Cynnie and I shared an apartment with another couple—hardly luxury accommodations.

It was a pretty sorry place; but we were together, and in that sense it was wonderful. Then the word came in. The company was shipping out. Destination: somewhere in France. I could only think back to my impressions of the German invasion of Poland, as an 18-year-old first walking the paths of Cornell. Little had I realized that one day I'd be going to Europe, as an American soldier, to fight in the war that had then just started.

We left on a transport from Boston in January 1945. The crossing was uneventful, if a little rough; the hard part was controlling your thoughts, and I wasn't fully successful. It was hard not to think that I might be making a one-way voyage to Europe. And would tonight be the night a German torpedo would slam us amidships and send us all to the bottom?

It was a relief, of sorts, when we arrived in Le Havre. I say "of sorts." We were now in a war-ravaged country, and the fighting was far from over, even though the Allied Forces, which had landed at Normandy on June 6 of the previous year, were advancing through France. But terra firma is terra firma, and a foot soldier feels better when his feet are on the ground. We were the 89th Infantry Division, Third Army, under the command of General George Patton.

Our job, to start, was to set up a camp near Rouen, which we named "Camp Lucky Strike." It was here we got ready for combat, and that basically meant marching, marching and more marching, getting used to the terrain and the weather, building up stamina. It rained every single day that first month. That crummy apartment Cynnie and I had shared with another couple at Camp Butner? In my mind's eye it was suddenly the Ritz!

The Germans had broken through the Allied front in the Belgian Ardennes in December of 1944, and had pushed successfully toward Antwerp. But now, in mid-January, the tide was turning in the Battle of the Bulge, and between forces led by Field Marshall Montgomery from the north and forces under General Patton from the south, the Nazi offensive was sputtering.

This was heartening news to those of us at Camp Lucky Strike. My unit, Group A Gun Group, set out shortly afterward for the front lines. We crossed the Moselle River, cleaning up pockets of Germans as we advanced. During this push, I was with a forward observation team; we were ahead of the front lines and radioed back any sightings we'd make of enemy forces. It wasn't trench warfare but it was dangerous duty, requiring nerves of steel. We were an isolated unit, easy prey if cornered or ambushed. As German shells screeched overhead, I often thought of Cynnie. And of our baby who had died. In those moments in France with death so frequent a visitor, how often I wished that our child had lived. Just in case…

A shell rocketed westward.

Spring came to the countryside, and the news was good. The Germans were losing, the war was coming to an end. But none of us would really believe it until it actually happened. One day, in a small French village, almost totally destroyed, I was walking with a French girl, perhaps 16 years old, who seemed lost and bereft. I tried to comfort her and handed her a piece of a chocolate from my rations just as a 1st lieutenant came riding up in a jeep with his driver.

We were all well aware of the strict rules against fraternizing with French civilians. We were allowed to walk and talk with them in the towns or along the road, but we could not accept any invitations into their homes. The lieutenant was the Officer of the Day and, charged with looking for infractions, accused me of fraternizing with the girl, of having been in her home. When I denied it he called me a liar.

A number of things worked on me all at once. I was dog tired, the stress of warfare was getting to me: I missed Cynnie and often wondered if I'd ever see her again. And I didn't like being called a liar. In the military, especially in wartime conditions, an enlisted man did not cross a field officer. If I said anything back, I would be opening myself up to a court martial, administered then and there possibly. But I did say something, perhaps unwisely. I said: "Get out of that jeep, take off those silver bars, and I'll show you who's a liar!"

The young lieutenant thought it over for several long seconds; then he motioned to his aide to drive on.

My closest call came just a few days before the war in Europe ended. My observation unit had just pulled into a French courtyard in which half a dozen big army trucks, 6x6s, were parked. I was standing with the company commander, Captain Gaylord, by one of the trucks, when a German shell came roaring in. I knew the sound; it was an 88. Just in time I fell to the ground, yelling at the other men to drop. Captain Gaylord, and others, were seriously injured, but I escaped without a scratch.

May 8th, 1945. V-E Day!

Back we went to Camp Lucky Strike. The second time around it wasn't so rough. We readied troops for new duty in the Pacific, and processed German POW's, and played a good deal of poker. Unlike the vast number of men who played poker in the service, I was one of the few who came out in the black. In fact, I won so regularly at our little quarter-limit games that I was able to live on those winnings and send all of my service pay back home to Cynnie in White Plains.

Shortly before we were shipped home, I had my best night ever. Abandoning my usual self-control, I got in a no-limit crap game, and won everything! I broke the bank, took all the money away with me, and never shot craps again. My buddies (some didn't stay my buddies) hollered for days, wanting a chance to win some of their money back, but I knew I'd had all the luck I was going to get. That money— $6,000—was already on its way back home where it would greatly ease my re-entry into civilian life.

But I did more than gamble during my spare time. It was a good period for reading and reflection. Several things kept coming back to me. One of them was how quickly I had chosen that single share of Lyon-Raymond stock over the $100 in cash my father had offered me on my twenty-first birthday. Another was my growing feeling that, in college, I was not really learning anything that would have a practical application for what I wanted to do—work for my father and take over the business when it came time for him to retire. Still, I wasn't entirely sure. Education, by and of itself, was a beautiful thing. I only had one more year at Cornell. Perhaps I should finish...

Then, as if he were psychic, my dad wrote me a letter, asking me what my plans were. Would I be going back to Cornell or coming back to the company? His three-page, single-spaced letter was quite a document. Every line said, in one way or another, it's your decision, do what you really think is best. Don't let me influence you in the least. But in between every line it was easy to hear him saying, "Come back to the family business!"

Which I decided, then and there, I would.

My ship home landed in New York. Five thousand GIs got off, all milling around the huge pier, awaiting orders. I was one of them. No civilians anywhere to be seen. Just soldiers. Suddenly, as if I were dreaming, I heard a woman's voice, a woman's familiar voice. "Have you seen Sergeant Raymond?"

I turned. Not ten feet away was Cynnie! I had to be dreaming. We ran into each other's arms, and I still thought it, I'm dreaming! When I finally got around to asking her how she had managed to get onto the pier—the only civilian and the only woman in the vast throng—she gave me a wily smile. She'd gone to the Navy Yard, asked permission, they had flat out denied it, she had persisted—and finally they just gave up and let her in. Never underestimate the power of a woman. Cynnie had convinced me of it once and for all.

After mustering out at Ft. Dix, I picked Cynnie up in White Plains and we promptly hopped on a train on the Delaware Lackawanna line for Binghamton, then up to Greene. When we stepped off, I knelt and kissed the earth. I was home.

Cynnie's parents gave us three acres on their farm, where we'd had the wedding, and we promptly set about building a house. Two bedrooms, living room, dining alcove, kitchen, bath—for a grand total of $9,875. While it was under construction, we stayed with my parents on S. Chenango Street.

One day, not long after I'd started working again at an annual salary of $4,560, I interrupted my father in his Greene office as he was telling me how unbiased the letter he'd sent me overseas was; he even claimed he'd had his top executives read it to make sure he wasn't trying to "twist George's arm."

I couldn't sit there and keep my mouth shut. "Sorry, Dad. It was totally biased in favor of the company over Cornell."

As proof, I handed him the letter. He read it, shook his head, smiled. "You know what, George?" he said. "You're right."

We both enjoyed a good laugh.

My father had steered the business through the war years by his wise procurement of a couple of government contracts, an area he'd never been in before. With the help of what he called a "tip"—an article in *Kiplinger's Washington Report* stating that there would be a demand for parts made from steel and other basic materials—he had scurried around and got several small contracts that, taken together, were enough to keep us afloat during the war years. My father downplayed his accomplishment, but there were an awful lot of other businessmen who read that same article and never won any contracts.

When the war had started, Lyon-Raymond was making products that could have easily been adapted for military use. Hand lift trucks, portable elevators, hand pallet trucks, and a lot of special equipment, such as cargo loaders for airplanes. In fact, in 1941 the company built the first baggage handler capable of taking cargo from the floor of the airport to the belly of an airplane, powered by a Ford tractor. American Airlines just loved it, but they wanted Lyon-Raymond to streamline its design, manufacture it, and charge half the price of what the company wanted for it. We were asking $4,500, and it had cost us $7,500 to build. Wisely, Lyon-Raymond bowed out. As it developed, a competitor in material handling, Rapid-Standard, built a similar baggage handler for American Airlines and ended up losing its shirt.

I'd been working for my father for almost a year, in my former slot as sales manager, when hardship and tragedy once again befell Cynnie. She learned she had a mastoid infection. Her physician in Binghamton said that while there was no real problem, it would prob-ably be best to operate, a decision that was to have dire consequences. We agreed that she would undergo surgery the following Monday morning at eight.

On Monday at seven I walked Cynnie into the operating room. I asked the doctor, a friend of mine, how long it would take, and he said two to four hours. I hadn't been in the waiting room for thirty minutes when I heard my name called over the intercom. I had a phone call.

It was from Cynnie's mother, who informed me that her husband, Cynnie's father, had died during the night. He had been in ill health for some time so it was not entirely unexpected.

I got word to the surgeon, but he had already begun the operation. We decided that the surgery should proceed. He told me how much time he thought I had until he would be finished, so I drove back to Greene, and, comforting Cynnie's mother as best I could, helped her make arrangements. Then I raced back to the hospital in Binghamton—and received the second bad blow of the morning.

The surgeon told me that he had discovered a growth on a major facial nerve, and that in removing it he had nicked the nerve, which, in effect, meant she no longer had any working nerves on one side of her face.

My wife, my beautiful Cynnie—how much pain, how much tragedy would she have to endure in her life? It was all too unbelievable. I sat down, having to bury my face in my hands. The surgeon said he'd told her about her face, but nothing about her father.

The damaged nerve could be repaired; well, that was something. But there were only two doctors in the northeast area who could perform the operation, one in Syracuse and the other in New York City, and it had to be done within five days. I chose his colleague in Syracuse, and arranged for an ambulance to take my wife there the following day.

The doctor in Syracuse turned out to be a grizzled veteran of the Army medical corps with hundreds of operations behind him. He told us bluntly, "I can't guarantee improvement, but I've done many, many similar operations. I keep track of all my patients, and every one of them has improved. Oh, by the way," he added, "I'm doing this as a favor to your doctor in Binghamton, who's a friend of mine too. There'll be no charge." Since the normal cost of the surgery was $5,000, I was greatly relieved and thankful.

Two days after the operation, Cynnie's mother got to see her daughter, whose head was wrapped so heavily she looked like something out of King Tut's tomb. By now the family had already buried Cynnie's father. My poor wife took one look at her mother and knew what had happened.

In the months immediately following the operation, Cynnie had to go to Syracuse for special electrical treatments on her face, and then later she was able to administer them to herself, at home. To our great relief, the operation was a success, and she regained perhaps three-fourths of her former appearance.

A year after her treatments finally ended, she confided to me that her greatest dread during the recovery period was that she would lose her looks and I would leave her. I took her in my arms, touched by her sweetness and her all-too-human fears. If she had told me sooner, I said, I would have convinced her that I would never leave her, no matter what. We were husband and wife. As I had said to her on a previous sad occasion, that meant for better or for worse.

On March 15, 1947, Cynnie was due to deliver a baby, and on that same date the engineers at the plant were to introduce a new lift truck, a major breakthrough in the industry. For the better part of the next thirty-six hours, I raced from plant to hospital and back, not knowing which birth would take place first.

I was nervous about both, but considerably more nervous about the baby. As it developed, I was present at the birth and the unveiling. Both were great successes, one coming into this world as a perfect human being, the other as a great engineering feat. The child was named George Gamble Raymond III. The machine was called the Lyon-Raymond L2P Hand Pallet Lift Truck.

Two years later, Cynnie and I were blessed with another trouble-free delivery—son number two, Stephen Spencer Raymond. Four years after that, when our daughter, Jean Crombie Raymond was born, it was also a blessed and worry-free event. As the memory of the war years faded, my wife and I, like so many other young couples in America, were enjoying what would come to be called "the greatest years."

In 1948, in honor of his twenty-fifth anniversary as owner-operator of Lyon-Raymond, my father produced a small booklet. He dedicated it to his wife, my mother. He wrote, "In recognition of her loyalty and continuing interest, her years of hard work, cooperation, and intuitive suggestions in helping to make this business grow, I dedicate this booklet to my wife, Madeleine C. Raymond."

It included a history of the town as well as the company, and there was another item of special interest: a picture of three male Raymonds. The caption beneath it read: "Three generations—George G. Raymond Sr., George G. Raymond Jr., and George G. Raymond III. George III, born March 15, 1947 is already preparing for the company roster and in due time is scheduled to carry on the future efforts of the company."

My father's lifelong dream, to own and run a family business, had come true years earlier. Now he had its future leaders all lined up.

3

From 'George, Jr.' to 'Mr. President'

Immediately after I rejoined Lyon-Raymond as a returning veteran in 1946, my father named me "Assistant to the President." One of my best friends, Stan Bryant, was sales manager, the job I'd had before enlisting.

Assisting my father wasn't a well-defined job; I did anything he asked me to. I was a "gofer," perhaps a glorified one but still a "gofer." No problem. I loved having a job in the company, living in my own house with Cynnie. Just being a civilian again was wonderful! Everyone's sleeves were rolled up, none higher than mine.

Everyone at work pitched in, eager to have the company flourish. Usually the rewards were great, but there were disappointments and setbacks. In the spring of 1947, my father, Stan, and I boarded a train in Binghamton. We were headed for the Material Handling Show in Cleveland, with my mother along for the trip.

As far as trade shows go, this one was not just a biggie; it was the biggie. It ran for a full week, and it was attended by manufacturers and their dealers and agents, plus customers and dealers from all over the country, Canada, and around the world. Stan and I set up the Lyon-Raymond booth and worked in it from early morning to well into the evening, and then we took people out for dinner and drinks.

As usual in our industry, this event was a very "liquid" affair, and it was a rare night that ended before 3:00 A.M. For the most part Stan and I joined in, seeing it as our job to make sure our clients and potential customers were enjoying themselves. To remain aloof would have been poor business. Plus it was good fun. If tiring.

By 6:00 P.M. on Friday, Stan and I were exhausted. We had the booth and the displays and everything we'd brought with us from the factory all packed up, tagged, and ready to ship. All we could think of was the comfort of that train ride home.

The station was directly beneath the Hotel Cleveland, where the company had booked a top-floor suite for the entire week—my parents in one bedroom and Stan and I in the other—and he and I went up to pack. Instead of finding my mother and father having a quiet drink, we walked in on my father, mother and our Cincinnati dealer talking in the living room. We sat down but didn't say very much because it was soon obvious that the dealer, a great old friend of my father, was plastered. Finally, my dad—and I had to admire the skillful way he did it—talked the dealer into leaving, and actually helped him over to the elevator. There was no way he would have made it on his own.

Stan and I sighed with relief. We would now be able to have a nice talk with my father and mother, get my father's views on how the show had gone, and have a general postmortem on the whole week. But when my father came back into the living room he was upset. He told us, in no uncertain terms, that we should have been nicer to the drunken dealer, should have joined in the conversation instead of letting my father carry it by himself, and definitely should have gotten up and walked with him and the man to the elevator.

We were both stunned. But my dad wasn't through. He continued ripping into us, laying us out in lavender, and finished with, "You're both fired!"

I was shocked. Here we'd just finished working the longest week we'd ever worked, had given 110 percent to the company, and because we didn't humor some drunk dealer we were fired? I was so mad, and hurt, that I went directly to my room where I threw my suitcase together, went downstairs, checked out, and got on the train. Tossing my bag in my roomette, I headed for the club car, where I ordered two double manhattans. The train wasn't scheduled to leave for another hour and twenty minutes, but I didn't care. I just wanted to sit there alone, mull over what had just occurred, and figure out what I was going to do next.

I was working on my second manhattan, when who should come along but Stan, a big grin plastered on his face.

"What are you smiling about?" I asked, sourly.

"I just got re-hired—with a raise!"

Now I was really mad. I polished off my second drink and went to bed. I walked into my office the next morning and started clearing out my desk. I took pictures and plaques—and my framed share of Lyon-Raymond stock—off the walls. I was just about finished when my father walked in, and said, "What in hell are you doing?"

I said, "Well, you fired me, so I'm leaving."

"Don't be ridiculous," he said, "you're not fired. Get to work."

I waited for him to say something else, along the lines that had made Stan so happy; but he never did.

I don't want to give the impression that I didn't enjoy working for my father or that he was some kind of cold-hearted dictator. He was an autocrat nonpareil, but he wasn't mean or vindictive. He simply liked running the show, the entire show. Lyon-Raymond was his baby. He nourished it, disciplined it, and, yes, caressed it, on a daily basis. He was a fair man, a tough but fair man.

My dad was a businessman through and through, and he never took his eye off the ball. I loved working for him, even though, from time to time, he came down hard on his employees; forget what my name was, I was one of them. I felt, more than anyone, the brunt of his autocratic ways. Maybe he was testing my mettle, seeing if I could withstand the pressure, looking hard at what his only son was made of. I did not want to disappoint him or let him down, and I worked hard, liking the fact that it was the family business I was helping him run, and hopefully learning to run. It was a rare day that I didn't get up eager to go to work.

As the years went on, my father gave me more and more authority over all areas of the business except one—the spending of money for capital improvements. That, after all, was the master key, and only one person at Lyon-Raymond had the authority to turn it.

In the fall of 1949 my father and I changed the name of the company. It was the natural progression from the original name, Lyon Iron Works. Our plan all along was to change our name in three steps, not wanting the public to think we dropped "Lyon" too quickly. It was a proud and exciting day for everyone when my dad and I took down the old Lyon-Raymond sign over the main entrance and put up the new sign. We were now "The Raymond Corporation."

Three months later, in early December of that year, my father took ill.

The man who was never sick, who rarely missed a day of work, started to complain of a persistent pain in his side. After a while it got better, but then it came back again, worse than before. Finally, in late December, he had to be hospitalized for exploratory surgery. When the surgeons in Binghamton opened him up they discovered that he was suffering from acute pancreatitis. I asked the chief surgeon what the prognosis was, and he said, simply, "It's not good."

"Give me the odds," I said.

"One in 10,000."

When I went in to see my father the following day, he could barely speak. He had tubes attached to every part of his body as he lay,
immobilized, in his hospital bed.

I couldn't tell him what the surgeon had told me, and I certainly
didn't tell him how scared I was. And I was scared. It was hard for me
to envision life without my father. He was my anchor to windward,
someone I could always go to, someone I could depend on.

But I was scared for another reason as well. Here I was, twenty-
eight years old, suddenly faced with the daunting task of running a
company that my father owned and ran with an iron hand. I remembered my fears when I'd first entered Cornell, wondering if I could
make the grade. I was wondering it again now, but in a much larger,
broader way.

I knew my father as well as I knew anybody, and I was sure he
would fight to his very last breath. He promised he would take it easy
for as long as he had to. Pleased by that, I suggested he go to St.
Petersburg on the west coast of Florida, where my mother's sister and
her husband had a place, and recuperate in the sun.

"I hate Florida, I could never live there," was his feisty response.

"How do you know that?" I asked. "You've never been down there
but a day or two at a time."

He admitted that was true, and with the urging of family members
and plant workers, he agreed to give it a try. To our surprise, he liked
Florida so much that he stayed there for almost a year. And he was
defying those odds. After such a dismal prognosis, it almost seemed a
miracle. If I hadn't known it before, I began to see what a tough
cookie my old man was.

An interesting and telling thing happened the very next day, a
Monday, after I visited my father in the hospital that first time. It had
been standard practice for years that each morning his top people

would come into his office and get their marching orders for the day. First it would be Bill House, vice president of manufacturing, who'd been with the company since the 1920s. Bill would go in and have ten or fifteen minutes with Dad, and when he'd come out, Chris Gibson, the chief engineer, would go in. After Chris, Stan Bryant, the sales manager, had his turn. Then Bill Lamb, the chief financial officer, followed by the production manager, Howard Murray. Because I was always in and out of his office as I pleased, as both his chief assistant and son, I knew what happened when these men came in each morning. My father would listen to them and to their ideas of what they should do that day, and he would never say a thing. But each one of them knew from the look on my father's face whether it was a yes or a no. Nobody ever made a mistake on that.

To my surprise, on that first Monday after my father's hospitalization, these same men, in the same order, trooped into my office and said, "George, Jr., this is what I propose to do today," and concluded by asking, "Should I?"

I simply told them to use their own good judgment: "If you think that's the right thing to do, then go ahead." Obviously they all had to have some sort of go-ahead before they felt comfortable enough to proceed.

That's how much of an autocrat my father was. He might have been in a hospital bed in Binghamton or on the patio of a house in Florida, but he was still there behind the big desk in his office, the captain's bridge from which he ran the good ship Raymond.

My father's recuperation surpassed everyone's hopes, and he came back to the company the next year. But it was clear from the start that he had no intentions of working with the verve and drive he'd always had. The illness had slowed him down, and he spent a good deal of time in Florida. In the everyday running of the business, he took a back seat, but in important company issues he still played a major role.

In 1949 I met an industry consultant in Philadelphia named Harry Messerole, who had been voted "Grocery Warehouse Consultant of the Year," which was quite a big deal in our industry. Messerole had an idea for a battery-powered forklift truck capable of handling single-faced pallets and stacking them two pallets high. This truck was designed specifically for small, multi-storied warehouses. But of even greater significance, Messerole's truck could be used in very narrow aisles. He had tried to convince people in the lift-truck business that this concept, which up until then existed only in his mind, had money-making potential. They all told him it would never work, it was a bad idea, forget about it. In short, nobody would touch it.

One day early in the next year, Chris Gibson, our chief engineer, and I were in Philadelphia on business. Our Philadelphia dealer, who happened to be a friend of Messerole's, convinced us to go see him and listen to his idea. We did, and Messerole showed us a series of drawings of the lift truck he'd envisioned. I was sufficiently intrigued that I told Harry we'd think about it, and I took a copy of the drawings back to Greene.

Well, Messerole kept bugging us and bugging us, and finally one day I asked Chris if he thought we could make this thing.

"I don't see why not," he replied.

"Could you design it?"

"Sure."

"Okay," I said, "do it. Make us a battery-powered narrow-aisle forklift."

Chris Gibson gave me a questioning look. "What about your father? Do I need his permission?"

I heard myself say, "Just do it. I'll worry about Dad."

And he started in. I watched him sketch each line, saw the production through from beginning to end, and when I saw the final result I liked it so much that I immediately got on and drove it.

Compared to what was available in the industry, this lift truck was compact, very "narrow aisle," highly maneuverable, and extremely strong. Its motive power was electricity—it had a huge battery—and it looked and handled like a sports car in a parking lot full of tractor-trailers. We saw a great future for it. Here's how good it was: Typically, a grocery warehouse of that period used 60 percent of the interior space for aisles, the rest for storage; with our new "narrow-aisle" truck, those figures were reversed: 60 percent usable space, 40 percent for aisles. It was every warehouse manager's dream come true.

There was a growing company down in Endicott, New York, twenty miles south of Greene, called International Business Machines. I had sold them a good many products in the past. I took the "Little-Lift-Truck-That-Could" to them and said, "Give it a field test for three or four or five months, just knock the hell out of it, and then tell me if it does the job."

They reported back in two months, "Your truck doesn't know the word 'quit.' We love it!"

If ever there was a happy marriage of product and customer, it was that of the Raymond narrow-aisle lift truck and IBM. We sold them several trucks of that same model, and many more of later models. Orders from other companies began coming in. From that point on, the narrow-aisle lift truck, proudly painted our signature shade of orange, became Raymond's signature product.

Some five years after my father's recuperation I was still receiving key personnel into my office each morning. My father had named me president of the company in 1953, and I had a great deal of work to do in my new position—I was virtually "in charge." But I was so busy answering questions or listening to ideas on a daily basis that I wasn't getting my own work done. More and more I realized that this was no way to run a railroad—or a factory. Problem was I didn't know what to do, how to alter the routine. I needed help. If I'd gone to my father, he would have said, "Well, George, it worked for me."

Luckily, I caught a break—or perhaps a shooting star—when I ran into someone I'd known for a long time at the American Management Association in New York. His name was George Brockway, and I had always respected him greatly. He had a mind that spun like a top and threw off ideas by the score.

He had lost his job with Rapid-Standard, a manufacturer of conveyor systems, because he and the CEO had not seen eye to eye, and he'd moved on to become a consultant to A.M.A., in whose offices we were now standing. After telling me about his position at American Management, he said, "I've got a little free time, George. Is there anything I can do for you?"

He didn't need to ask twice.

George Brockway came to Greene the next month, and after sitting in my office on Monday morning for an hour or two, and watching the "parade," he suggested we walk down the street to the Elm Tree and get a cup of coffee. When we were seated in the little restaurant, he said, "How do you get any work done?"

"I don't, that's just it."

"George, listen to me," he said, "the answer's very simple. Starting tomorrow, tell each of your morning 'visitors' you'll no longer see them every day. You'll see one of them on Monday morning, another on Tuesday, and a third on Wednesday, and so on. You'll see each executive once a week"—he stressed the phrase—"but you'll give each of them all the time they want. In between, if they have a question they can't answer, they're to call you on the phone. They are not to come into your office."

Well, that little bit of restructuring worked like a charm. In just two weeks, individuals, once so dependent on the "go ahead," were taking on responsibilities they never would have dreamed of before, and I was getting my work done in a timely fashion.

Even though I wasn't fully aware of it at the time, thanks to George Brockway I had just passed the first milepost on the journey toward managerial attitude change. I had taken a significant step on the road to my way of running the company.

So pleased was I with Brockway's performance, vision and ideas that in 1956 I hired him for a key role in the company. Of course I didn't do it without consulting with my father. In fact, I made a special trip to Florida, with George, for this purpose. While my dad, who had known Brockway for years and liked him very much, approved the hiring, he didn't buy my idea of giving Brockway the title of executive vice president. It took a lot of doing on my part, but I finally talked him into it.

Two pairs of documents from those early days shed a great deal of light on the fundamentally different ways—perhaps even diametrically opposed—my father and I thought a company should be run. They also shed light on our different personalities.

The first is a letter he wrote when he got out of the hospital and was about to leave for Florida to recuperate.

To the Grand People at the Plant:

I want to thank you a million for the messages in various forms to cheer me up, which I received from many of you while I was in the Binghamton City Hospital.

After twenty-nine days of it, much of which was not too bad, my first thrill was to take several deep breaths of nice fresh air before I stepped into the car (under my own power, thank God!) bound for home. It was a delightful ride home and Greene looked awfully, awfully good to me. I had the pleasure of riding by the Plant, and, believe me, I wanted to get out and come in to say hello to all of you personally but that was not on my doctor's schedule; however, I am looking forward to that pleasure.

Last evening Madeleine and I celebrated Christmas by opening the gifts which we had received. Among them was the very lovely card that was signed by all of my very good friends at the Plant. This is going to stand high among all the presents that I cherish the most. The verse was very touching and I would like to duplicate the card in its entirety. I wish that all of you could have a card just like the original; as the best substitute that I can think of, I am attaching a sheet with the thoughts expressed on the card, together with a list of all of the signatures. I think we all can be very happy and proud to be one of such a grand group.

Before hitting the hay, Madeleine remarked that even though it was late, it was one of the grandest Christmas celebrations we have ever had. I thoroughly agreed with her and we both want to thank you from the bottom of our hearts for helping to make it such a pleasant one.

Sincerely, George

Attached to the letter was a sheet that contained three single-spaced columns of names, 101 in all (including mine), and this poem, also by my father:

CHRISTMAS GREETINGS, "SPECIAL FRIEND"

Once in a while a friend is found
Who's a friend right from the start,
Once in a while a friendship's made
That really warms the heart,
Once in a while a friendship's formed
To last a lifetime through,
It really does happen,
Just once in a while—
It happened to me and you.

MERRY CHRISTMAS AND HAPPY NEW YEAR

A pair of considerably longer documents was written three and a half years later by an outside consulting firm. I first heard of the firm through George Brockway in 1953, when he'd worked for Rapid-Standard. By chance, we were both visiting a dealer in Cleveland on the same day—and a discussion came up about a company that provided psychological services to industry. Worthington Associates had just appraised the strengths and weaknesses of a prospective salesman for R-S. Because of my growing interest in behavioral science as it applied to business management I thought it might be a good idea to bring Worthington Associates to Greene.

Of course I didn't present Worthington to my father in that same light. Instead, I told him we could use their services in evaluating potential salespeople. I showed him some of their literature, and he said, "Let's have them do an evaluation of our management. We know who we have and how they perform, and if their evaluation matches what we already know, then maybe I'll use their service."

A couple of months later Worthington came to the company, and together they devised a long questionnaire. Then they did all sorts of interviews, and finally they produced a report. Actually, Worthington Associates produced two reports dated December 3, 1953. The first was an evaluation of the company as run by my father, and the second was an evaluation of me.

THE MANAGEMENT STRUCTURE
OF THE RAYMOND CORPORATION

PRESENT AND FUTURE

Before going into the discussion of the seven men who submitted Personal Histories and Incomplete Sentence Series, it seems worthwhile to lead off with some discussion of George G. Raymond, Sr. While we do not have any direct information on him, it is possible to make inferences about him as a person and as an executive from the knowledge we have of the company and of the other members of the executive team. It should be emphasized that these are only inferences; and we may be wrong on some major points. However, he plays such a central role in the company, and in the lives of the executives of the company, that we consider it necessary to make these inferences if we are to be of maximum service.

Mr. Raymond is undoubtedly the inspiration, the chief salesman, the source of most of the ideas which have been put into practice, and generally the sparkplug of the firm. He is a decisive executive, who has taken upon himself the major responsibility for almost all, if not all, departments of the company. Chiefly because of his ability and his personal investment in building the company, his is the deciding voice, and this fact has been recognized and accepted by his staff. The senior officers of the company have probably habitually deferred to his judgment even in matters quite central to their own areas of responsibility. Usually this has been done without begrudging him this prerogative; and they certainly are not "yes men." It has been recognized that his judgment has almost without exception been sound. In addition, he has managed to "encroach" on their responsibility without putting them on the defensive by ignoring their ideas or judgments. He is genuinely interested in their opinions and has faith in their judgment as well as pride in their competence. However, he has felt so intensely that the company was *his*—his life, his career, in some respects his "baby"—that he has not really seen a need to delegate complete and final authority to any members of his staff. Because he has been such a dynamic and foresighted executive, he has been primarily responsible for the company's rapid growth and sound condition, and this is generally understood by his staff.

His attitude toward his employees has been very much that of the father toward his children, with all that is thus implied. The children of a forceful, effective, and loving father are quite willing to accept his exercise of power over their lives, with the feeling that their futures are secure in his hands. They will admire and respect him; they will have faith and trust in him. However, precisely because of his effectiveness and his positive attitudes, they will experience difficulty in escaping from his influence, in becoming independent adults, in making their own way in the world. Such a father has to help his children to free themselves of his too pervasive influence. He has to help them to stand on their own feet, to make their own decisions, to come to trust their own ability to fulfill their responsibilities. This must be a positive program on his part. To just cast them adrift would only make them uncertain and fearful. They must grow from adolescents into completely adult men *with* his help and *with* his encouragement. This general "formula" has specific applications to The Raymond Corporation.

The high caliber of the executives of the company is the best evidence of the personal effectiveness of Mr. Raymond, Sr. (There are only one or two exceptions.) The fact that he has gathered such men about him indicates that he is not afraid of competition and has no need to be "the boss" in the hostile sense of that word; that he has no need to "cut men down to size." He has demonstrated in the most telling way that he is willing and eager to get the best men he can to work with and under him. He has given them loyalty and support as well as personal interest and attention. It is apparent that the executives have deep feelings of gratitude, loyalty and affection for him. (This applies with greatest force, of course, to those who have been with the company for some time. The newer men are still "feeling their way around" and do not have such firm convictions.)

WORTHINGTON PERSONAL HISTORY ANALYSIS

PERSONAL CHARACTERISTICS of GEORGE RAYMOND JR.

Energy Work Attitudes

George is a very capable man who has not yet fully developed his potentialities for independent action and decision as a top policy-making executive. Partially because of limited experience, he sometimes undervalues his own abilities and is not really sure that he is as capable as he actually is. Puts a great deal of energy into proving himself in his work. Will be able to accomplish more, when he has attained a fuller sense of personal competence in directing actual operations on his own. His father has set a strong example for him. Unconsciously, he tends to compare his own performance with that of his father, particularly in manners and styles of dealing with executive problems. Can feel slightly disappointed with himself if he thinks he has not handled an important matter in quite the same way that he knows his father would, even when the end results are highly creditable.

He would benefit greatly from being able to compare his ability with executives from other corporations in an experience such as a high level management-training course. When he realizes and accepts the fact that, although his modus operandi is naturally somewhat different from his father's, he is perfectly capable of getting good results in his own way, he will function much more easily, more confidently, and more effectively.

Emotional Stability Ambition Self-regard

George is reaching out to become a completely mature master of adult tasks and roles. At the moment, he is somewhat concerned about how he will fit into the corporate structure when his father retires from active management. Wonders if he can earn and hold the respect of his colleagues, by and for himself. Also, he is not completely certain of his ability to operate successfully on his own. Does not recognize that he is quite capable of making adequate final business decisions, here and now. Some of his hesitation and occasional impulsive error stems from his ambivalence about assuming authority. While he feels capable of doing so, he is not sure that he has the right to do it. Consequently, he is sometimes a little impulsive and sometimes over-cautious in his efforts to do his best. Can move in too hastily, make a rapid beginning that requires minor shifts after he sees the direction his initial actions are taking. This gives him some sense of strain, which is not objectively necessary. Aside from this, he is a friendly, honest, and unassuming man who has a relatively high degree of emotional stability and self-confidence.

He sees himself in the role of the good son and is content to function in that role while his father continues in active management. Partly as a function of this, but also in his own right, he has a natural concern for the company and its welfare. This is more important to him than any personal aggrandizement that might result from his high position. Feels a bit pushed, as though adult responsibilities had been given him before he was completely ready to undertake them. Nevertheless, he accepts the challenge and intends to prove his mettle. What he needs now, perhaps more than anything else, is an opportunity to sit down and quietly work out on his own terms, just who and what he is, as an individual, as a person apart from his family and corporate relationships. This might best be accomplished through a series of conferences with a skilled professional counselor who could facilitate his growing awareness of these major issues in his life....

This was my first taste of an outside, psychology-based corporate appraisal, and a pleasant enough taste it was—though there was some bitter and some sweet to it, obviously. If I hadn't bumped into George Brockway in Cleveland, my journey on the path of modern management would have been delayed or conceivably might never have begun.

What a dynamo he was! He'd breeze into my office, I'd close the door, and we'd talk. I'd sift through his ideas to get to the best ones, then we'd open my door and call all the top managers together and tell them what the company was going to do, the new direction it would be taking, how we'd be handling this situation or that.

Well, they didn't take to it one bit. However, they didn't tell me they disapproved; instead, they told my father! They did this secretly, but my father responded by calling me and saying he had named this group—that is, all the company officers who reported to me—as the Administrative Committee. Further, he had given it veto power over my, and George Brockway's, ideas!

I eventually learned that what bothered my father the most was that George and I would make all our plans with the door to my office closed. Doing this, I was quick to see, was a mistake. Quite understandably, suspicions that Brockway was "influencing" George Jr. abounded, and these distorted views were passed on to my dad. In a few words, he was not happy with "the George Brockway situation," while I thought George was a great addition to the company. Something had to give, and I saw my first boardroom "shootout" looming on the horizon.

Before that happened, my father and I made the decision in 1956 to go public with The Raymond Corporation. His chief reason for this was personal. He had recovered from his illness but was nervous about his health after his big scare. To solve an estate tax problem that would certainly arise at his death, he would have to have a source of money available. The only way to make his holding liquid, so he could sell shares, was to have an initial public offering. Also, we needed capital to finance our growth—we were building an all-new manufacturing facility on Wheeler Street in Greene. I knew it was the right way to go, and I urged my father to make the step. With the issuing of nearly two million shares over the counter, at $14 a share, my father's tax problems were resolved, and Raymond had the public backing to move forcefully ahead in the material-handling industry.

To everyone's surprise, my father enjoyed Florida so much that he bought a place of his own and started spending winters in the Sunshine State. But he always came up to vote in local and national elections, and for meetings of the Board of Directors.

At one such board meeting in 1957 he made the trip, as usual, and, characteristically bold and to the point, informed me that his first order of business would be to get rid of George Brockway. My father walked into the board meeting and, without even calling it to order, said, "We have to fire George Brockway. All in favor signify your vote by... "

"Wait a minute, Dad," I said, speaking up. "Let's discuss this first."

"As far as I'm concerned," he said, "there's nothing to discuss."

"I'd like to speak."

He told me to go ahead, and I came to George's defense. He was a great thinker with many innovative ideas, I said. The company was running better, our production was increasing, and we had tighter control of inventory. Plus sales were increasing: $5 million in 1955, $7.9 million last year, and this year we were headed for our best year yet. Brockway was partly responsible for this growth.

The instant I finished, my father said, "Okay, now vote."

Because I, not he, was responsible for the three non-family members on our board, and because, as board members, they were familiar with Brockway's excellent work in the company, I fully expected they would side with me; and that would be that. To my astonishment, they sided with my father, and by a vote of five to one, with chief engineer Chris Gibson abstaining, George Brockway was gone.

I was so mad I didn't trust myself to stay in the room, and stormed off to the men's room. One of the directors followed me in—Tom Wilson, a banker, a man my father's age whom I admired greatly.

When I was only eighteen, I'd gone with my dad to The Marine Midland Bank in Binghamton; he had wanted to open a line of credit. Trouble was, Mr. Wilson didn't see any record of earnings. My father said, "I don't want the line on what I have earned, I want it on what I'm going to earn." He got the loan.

"I suppose your first question," Tom said, "is why did three outsiders vote with your dad and not with you."

"It sure as hell is!"

"Let me tell you something," he said. "There are a number of family businesses in Binghamton. I'm on the boards of most of them, and I've saved several from going on the rocks. The trouble usually starts with a fight between father and son or brother against brother. Look, I heard your presentation, and it was clear you held the trumps. But if we had voted against your father, it would have split you and him right down the middle, and the company as well. He would never have gotten over it. He's too old but you're not. You're plenty young enough to get over it—and I suggest you start doing that right now."

He paused for a moment, laid a hand on my arm. "There are a lot of people out there who are just as good, as talented, as George Brockway. I suggest you start looking."

Fortunately, I had enough sense to listen to Tom Wilson and to take his advice. As for the relationship between my father and me, there was no damage done because he was never one to hold a grudge. As soon as he walked out of the board meeting, he'd forgotten it all. And me? I went back to my office and worked. George Brockway landed on his feet as a successful consultant, and he and I remained close friends until the day he died. Most of all, I'll never forget how helpful Tom Wilson was that day in getting me back on track and for giving me an important insight into a family business. It's often the outsider who has the best view.

4

The Greening of a CEO

My life had a happy balance in those days, a nice proportion between home and work. Cynnie and I had views much like those of all the other couples we knew in the 1950s: she took care of the home and I took care of the office. Business required me to travel about half the time to meet with our growing network of dealers, and to call on customers old, new, and potential. Our sons, Pete and Steve, were quite young then, and Jean was just a baby. Like so many fathers, I would see my kids on the weekends and of course during the summers at our cottage on Geneganslet Lake. Just as my father had done with me, I took the boys to the factory from time to time, and I recognized in them the excitement I'd felt when my father had taken me to his office, in what was becoming a distant past.

My most serious extracurricular activity at the time was with the local school board, and the issue that pressed me into service was the physical condition of our school building. In a word, it was rickety—so rickety that the principal, whom everyone in the community liked and respected, threatened to quit if we didn't get a new one. I took it upon myself to form a citizens' committee to study the issue and to lobby for a new building. The school board, a timid body if ever one existed, not only feared going to the State Regents committee chairman, who lived nearby, but also feared going to Albany to ask for a new building. Finally, one of the members persuaded me to go on their behalf. I agreed, making the trip with a solid presentation filled with facts, figures and photos, all of which showed that we needed— and deserved—a new K-12 building.

After a good deal of discussion, the Regents approved the request; they also said that our school board needed leadership. At home, I was urged to accept board membership, which I did, and in 1953 I was elected president of the school board, a position I held for twenty years.

Travel was quite different in those days. Whether it was for business or for pleasure, getting around was nothing like today. At first all my travel was by train; then I began taking American Airlines and other early carriers, most of which flew DC-3s on routes that sound ludicrous today. If I wanted to fly to Cleveland, I had to take a train to Buffalo, 160 miles away, to catch the plane. Turnpikes and interstates were still the dreams of visionary planners, so driving was slow and circuitous. Except for short trips in and around the Southern Tier, I would also take the train. I'd board on Sunday night and be gone until Friday. During that week I'd visit between three and six different cities. My territory was the entire United States and Canada, but because most of our business was north of the Mason-Dixon line and east of the Mississippi, I concentrated on that area.

The people I called on were part of our nationwide system of manufacturer's representatives, which had been built up by my father. If someone interested in sales wrote my father and convinced him that he could do a good job of representing the company, Dad gave him the chance. By the time I began to travel as sales manager in 1947, when Stan Bryant left the company, there was a good number of sales reps, about fifty-five in all, that I would visit in this country and Canada, and I would stop in and see as many as I could on any given "tour."

In those days, thanks to the Robinson-Patman Act of 1936, which was designed to foster competition, we couldn't give exclusive territories, so we got around it by awarding "preferred" territories, which amounted to the same thing. That lasted until the late 1950s, when we started marketing our new electric narrow-aisle lift truck. Because manufacturers' reps didn't have service facilities, we switched to a network of dealers who could service and repair the equipment.

For the most part, we kept the same reps, but we trained them thoroughly in all manner of repair work. For Raymond, service became a number one priority. We wanted our customers to know that we stood behind our products long after they left Greene; in short, we wanted them to trust us as a company. I had worked hard to establish a rapport with these men while they were reps, based on that same principle. They had come to trust me, to know I was a man of my word, and now they were working to develop trusting relationships with the lifeblood of any company—the customer. It was no wonder that our dealership system flourished.

The Worthington Report had said that while I may have been almost naive in trusting people as I did, that aspect of my nature would become an asset as I matured. Because Raymond dealers knew I would go to the wall for them, they would do the same for me.

One reason dealers liked me was that when I took over as sales manager, I scrapped my father's system of payment in favor of one that paid them more money, sooner, and also gave them more control over their livelihood. Under my father, dealers might have to wait for their commissions, sometimes a month or more. I changed that system. As soon as Raymond shipped a lift truck to the customer, the dealer was given his commission. And when the dealers wanted to form their own trade organization—MHEDA, for Material Handling Equipment Dealers Association—I encouraged them, something my father would have never done. It was already clear to me that I had to look down the road and keep my eye on the big picture, which meant helping the dealers get their own organization so they could become a force in the industry. As a result, it wasn't long before I had their complete loyalty.

When I became president of the company in 1953, I recognized the need to cut back on the number of Raymond dealers. With fewer dealers, I reasoned, the lines of communication between dealerships and company would improve. We would be able to give a reduced number of dealers broader responsibility. The company also guaranteed that no other Raymond dealer would be allowed in an existing dealer's territory. In the execution of this plan, we eventually reduced our dealerships from 55 to 30, with the biggest centers in New York, Chicago, Detroit, Cleveland, and Denver.

As our new narrow-aisle forklift caught on, its bright orange become the signature color of the entire Raymond Corporation. Our especially loyal and dedicated employees, were said to "bleed orange." It was said of me many times, and I always took it as the highest compliment.

The dealers became our best salesmen. We'd have customers come into the factory in Greene, and when we'd go to give them a pitch, they'd wave us away, saying, "We're already sold. Just take my order."

Our dealerships became central to the success of the company. They were so integral a part of our operation, that we began issuing "The Raymond Needle," a newsletter just for dealers and their salesmen, in which we poked fun at, informed, and (hopefully) entertained the "troops."

The first item in the May 13, 1953, issue was a note from me. It read:

Is my hat shrinking?? Just been promoted to President and the fit seems kinda snug. The promotion's fine, but still being bossed by Cynnie and the kids. Seriously... gonna continue to need the help and support you've given me in the past. More details from G.G.R., Sr., attached...

Other entries were directed more toward business:

DeWitt and George Adams just back from Super Market Show in Cleveland...Left the E4ST and L2P there.... Larry Hillis had 'em sold to Premier Autoware before the show even opened.... which is super fast sellin'.... Show (& our truck) created a lot of interest and some excellent inquiries.

And:

Don't want to sound like a Hollywood ad, but April sales were TERRIFIC! Biggest month in our entire history! You fellas did a great job and wish I could thank you each personally. Keep it up— I love to sign those fat commission checks.

I even tried my hand at humor:

"Fella was explaining what was the matter with his car: "The battery doesn't bat, spark plugs don't spark, and the pistons don't work either.""

Oh well...

In 1956, my father informed the board of directors that he would step down as chief executive officer of The Raymond Corporation in three years. And he specified that the board name me as his successor, which they did in January of 1959—I liked to think not only because my dad had asked them to, but because they believed I was up to the job.

Unlike several years earlier, when my father and mother surprised everyone, including me, by announcing that I was company president, this time I had no hesitation about accepting and no doubts as to whether I could do the job. I knew I could; after all, I'd had considerable practice. For all intents and purposes I'd held the top position since 1949, when my father took ill. I'd served my apprenticeship, paid my dues, and was deeply gratified when my father handed me the company's mantle of leadership.

The promotion to CEO brought with it one particularly welcomed change, the untying of the corporate purse strings. As ridiculous as it may sound, my father retained control over all capital expenditures in excess of fifty dollars while he was CEO. As president, I'd had the authority to hire a vice president for $25,000 a year, a fine salary in those days, but I couldn't spend $51 for a water cooler!

The evaluators from Worthington Associates were really on the mark when they wrote that I had not, as of 1953, developed my "potentialities for independent action and decision as a top policy-making executive," and that I didn't realize how capable I was. And they were certainly right in observing that George Jr. "tends to compare his own performance with that of his father and... can feel slightly disappointed with himself if he thinks he has not handled an important matter in quite the same way that he knows his father would, even when the end results are highly creditable."

The years from 1949 to 1956 were not my easiest period. Following his illness, and his discovery that much to his surprise he liked Florida, my father was still very much present at the company, even during the six winter months he and my mother spent down south. Although we had re-configured the offices, taking his and mine out of the main stream of managerial traffic, everyone knew where his office was and when he was "in." Interestingly, I think he believed that he no longer had any real power, that he had transferred it to me; and I believed that too. Problem was no one else did.

During that period, Dad would go to an officer of the company and, just out of curiosity, ask him a question, and the officer would take it as an order and do whatever he thought my father had asked him to do. As a result of this confusing practice by all the top executives, which really went on for five or six years, The Raymond

Corporation wobbled. Our sales stayed at about $5 million a year, and profits went up and down, until the early 1960s when profits began climbing. It was no coincidence that business, generally, started improving when managers realized that I was, in fact, the boss, and they didn't have to worry about what my father might think or say regarding any action they had taken at my direction.

That was not the only reason we started moving ahead in so decided a fashion. Instrumental was the fact that I made it clear—to others but mainly to myself—that I wanted to learn and grow. As a result of this realization, I entered a period in my life in which I was open and receptive to people who could help me go where I wanted, and needed, to go. The old adage, "When the student is ready, the teacher appears" was definitely true in my case.

My first real teacher had been George Brockway. George taught me how to delegate authority and to give responsibility to others. On a more concrete level, he showed me how to make a record of my new policies—and how to communicate them to others. We did this by writing *The Raymond Management Guide,* a document that broke down the president's job into thirty-two different and distinct functions, then laid them out in categories such as Objectives, Policies, Plans, Expected Results, and Controls. With a section for each function, this handy document became our bible. Unknowingly, I had taken my first step toward organizational development and team management. Looking at it in retrospect, this was also my first big step away from my father and his authoritarian methods.

When George and I first came up with this idea, I was concerned that my father wouldn't take to it, so we made a special trip down to Florida to show him the *Guide.* To my surprise, he barely glanced at what we'd written, saying, "Don't bother me. If this is what you want to do, then go do it. It's okay with me."

Well, maybe it was and maybe it wasn't, but shortly thereafter my dad formed the Administrative Committee, whose secret reports, based on suspicion more than fact, sealed Brockway's fate with the company. My father made his decision to fire him on bad information. Often, and unfortunately, that's the way it goes.

My next teacher of note was a man named Richard Beckhard, who would become one of the major mentors of my life, and such a close friend that I consider him my honorary older brother. But before bringing Dick on stage, I have to paint some scenery.

During World War II, while Ray Hickcock and his younger brother, of the now famous Hickcock Belt Company, were away in uniform, their father ran the company. It was doing fine, about $20 million a year. Then the father suddenly died, and the sons were given a "compassionate discharge" and sent home. The elder, Ray, took over the business. With the tremendous postwar demand for jewelry and accessories, the company started to do extremely well, but after a few years, when the demand waned, Hickcock needed to cinch up its own belt. Ray said to himself, I can't be the only guy in this particular boat; there must be others. So he looked around, found a number of "others," and suggested they get together and compare notes—at a hunting lodge in Canada he owned. They did, and out of that grew the Young Presidents' Organization.

When the media first heard of YPO and its genesis at Hickcock's hunting lodge, they made fun of the group as a bunch of rich young businessmen with nothing better to do than complain that their profits were slipping. But as the organization grew and prospered, it became clear this was a serious and viable group that knew what it was doing, and eventually the media coverage improved. When I first heard about the organization, I'd been president of Raymond for about three years, and knew in my bones I could use some help. But where to go for it?

I certainly wasn't going to go to my father and say, "Dad, I need to bolster my confidence. Do you know anybody in that business?" So when I heard about YPO, I was interested right away. In those days, in order to join the Young Presidents' Organization, you had to be under 40, and the president of a company with revenues of at least $1 million a year. But you couldn't just apply; you had to be put up for membership by two members, though a single no vote could keep you out. I contacted two Raymond dealers who happened to be members, and asked them to back me, and I made it on the first try. Joining YPO turned out to be one of the smartest things I ever did.

It was not a large organization in those days, but it happened to have two chapters in New York state. In order to attend a meeting of the Empire chapter, I had to drive from Greene to Rochester, a good two-hour trip. When I got there, I never had what I considered a stimulating time. Typically, I'd arrive, attend the lunch, and then someone would ask, "Anybody got anything to talk about?" Hardly anybody would, which meant the meeting was over, and back home I'd go.

After a few months of wasting time in this manner, I decided that instead of the chapter meetings I'd attend an area conference. The nation was divided into fifteen areas, each of which held a three-day conference once a year, and then there was a big national convention held annually. I started going to the area conferences, and found them much more stimulating and helpful. Pretty soon I was being asked to "volunteer" for such jobs as helping run an area conference. I did so, enjoyed it, and met some fine people, one of whom was Roger P. Sonnabend, the head of Lionel Trains and Sonesta Hotels. Roger was YPO's national president that year.

After my tentative start with the regional chapter, I became quite active in YPO and took full advantage of my membership, attending conferences on all levels and in a number of different cities. Despite the negative press the organization used to get about how much fun its members always had at meetings (especially the national conference), YPO was really all about learning. If you said, as I eventually did, that you wanted to learn how to improve in a certain area of management or interpersonal relationships, YPO was there to teach you.

That's how I ended up, in 1958, in New York City at a two-day training session on becoming a seminar leader, and that's where I met Dick Beckhard, one of the three experts putting on the session. That was the beginning of our association, which produced not just a business relationship of decades-long standing, but also a deep personal friendship.

Ironically, it was my wife, the ultimate non-joiner, who first got me involved in the entire self-awareness movement. Cynnie took after her parents, both of whom were reserved; she was not an outgoing person. Some family members on my side mistook that reserve for haughtiness, but I never saw it that way. She had her interests and her loves—home, children, gardening, golf—but when the kids were older she began to grow restless.

One day she announced she was tired of being "just a housewife." She wanted to "do something else." I mentioned that YPO had a wives' group, which, in fact, was about to hold a week-long conference in Washington, D.C. To my astonishment, she said she'd like to go, and—still shaking my head in disbelief—I made the arrangements.

If anyone had asked me, I would have said that Cynnie would be back in two days. She had never done anything like this before and, frankly, it was out of character. When I didn't hear from her on Monday, I was a bit surprised, and when I didn't hear from her the next day, I was very surprised. So, on Wednesday, I called her and asked how she was doing. She replied, in a rush, "Fine. Haven't time to talk. Bye."

On Thursday, it snowed heavily in Greene, so I phoned Cynnie Friday morning, worried she might have trouble getting a flight. "Don't give it a second thought," she said. "I'll take care of it myself." That too was unusual. There I was, offering help, and she had flat-out refused it!

I met her plane, and the minute she saw me she started talking—and wouldn't stop. She said the whole conference was wonderful, especially the sessions called "T-group"—the "T," she explained, stood for "training." She'd learned a lot about herself, why she was basically reserved and introspective, what her fears and ambitions were. I was fascinated by what she was saying. Later that evening, after we were safely inside our house—the drive home over snowy roads had been treacherous—Cynnie wondered, aloud, why T-Groups were only for women. Didn't they have something like that for men? "If they do," she urged, "you should attend one, George. I think you'd really get a lot out of it. I know one thing—I feel changed!"

As it turned out, YPO did offer such sessions for men, and there was one scheduled for the next month in Hudson, New York, less than a hundred miles from Greene. I signed up and at that meeting I again met Dick Beckhard and, as an added bonus, another dynamic man, Bob Blake.

Present at the Hudson workshop were fifteen people, split into two groups. Blake was the trainer of the group I was in, and Dick Beckhard led the other. A man named Norm was listed as a no-show, so we started without him. In essence, we engaged in a series of controlled confrontations designed to make each YPO member more aware of his strengths and weaknesses as a corporate leader. It was, I learned quickly, a self-development process.

We worked so hard and well in the first session that we all retired early. My roommate for the week was the CEO of Vicks, the

"Vapo-Rub" company. Ralph and I talked for about fifteen minutes in our room, then, simultaneously yawning, decided to turn in.

Well, at about 10:15, Norm finally showed. To our discomfort and annoyance, he burst into our room and said, in a voice resembling a bullhorn, "What the hell kind of a YPO meeting is this? You guys in bed already?"

Together we told him to leave; we were tired, we'd catch up with him in the morning.

Norm didn't take our comment well. "What are we suddenly, a bunch of Boy Scouts?"

"Just get the hell out," Ralph said.

Mumbling, he left. The next morning Norm came into the first session, right after breakfast, and said, loudly, "Sorry I wasn't able to get here on time. Now let's go around the table and each one of you tell me what I missed."

When the first person started in, Norm interrupted. "Oh, I know all about that," and did the same with the next two or three men.

At the coffee break, the chief executive of Vicks said to me, "We've got to shut this guy up! I don't care if he is the CEO of a *Fortune 500* company."

I agreed.

"I'll start it going," he said, "then you join in."

When we got back, Norm picked up right up where he'd left off, and Ralph wasted no time in keeping his word. "For Christ's sake," he said, "will you shut up and give the rest of us a chance?"

Before I could add a word, Norm, an anguished expression on his face, said, "Oh my God, am I doing it again?"

He then proceeded to tell us, sheepishly, that his company back home had a big, specially designed conference table, equipped with buttons purposely placed out-of-sight. In the middle of the table was a buzzer. If someone talked too long, all anyone had to do was give one of the buttons an anonymous hit with his knee, and the buzzer would go off.

I put the question to him: "Anyone but you ever get buzzed?"

"No," said Norm, laughing, "only me!"

He turned out to be a great guy, once we got through to him, and a very productive member of the T-group. A few years later I visited Norm's company, and sure enough there stood that infamous table, buttons, buzzer and all...

I attended one seminar in that early period where, purely by chance, several people started talking about the problems they had in common—as second-generation executives to run a family business. These problems involved conflicts they had with their fathers. I didn't have much to say, and as I walked out I felt a sense of relief and good fortune that their problems weren't mine. Sometimes my father would call me to task. I'd stormed out more than once on him, upset and angry. But when you had a relationship built on the bedrock of respect and love, as we did, it would see you through.

In 1962, it was the Empire Chapter's turn to run the Northeast area conference, a three day affair held in October. Normally, a member would be chosen at the spring meeting and given the opportunity to pick the site and do the advance planning, but this year the person who'd been tapped had backed out, and I got a call asking me if I would run it. I wanted to be active in YPO and move up the ladder, so I readily accepted.

Our area conference was to be held in Bermuda, at the Carleton Beach, a Sonesta hotel. As any member was free to attend any area conference, we thought that we'd draw a lot of members from other areas, especially the more northerly ones, because of our location in the dead of winter. Then we learned that the Eastern area had selected Washington, D.C. as the site for its meeting on the same dates as ours— and had been promised an appearance by President John F. Kennedy!

Knowing we had to come up with something good, we pulled out all the stops. One of the many tricks we used was to have sets of beautiful cufflinks made with the YPO logo. We sent one cufflink with the announcement and application form, and promised the other when (and if) the invitee showed up in Bermuda.

I and two other YPO members, who also had no experience running conferences, met for a three-day planning session, and I learned more than I'd ever known before about how to run a big, multi-day meeting. National YPO provided us with such a wonderfully detailed "book" on how to run a large group meeting—right down to the proper type and amounts of alcohol. It was so good that I brought it home with me and used it for company functions.

As a result of our efforts, we had a good showing of thirty couples in Bermuda. We met them at the airport with personalized tags for their luggage and goodie bags for the wives; among the items inside were gold charms for charm bracelets. (Cynnie eventually filled not one but three charm bracelets, courtesy of YPO.) We had cabs lined up and handed members their hotel keys as they got in their cabs.

The weather was beautiful when they arrived; then it rained for three solid days. We had planned an outdoor steak roast; the hotel said we could still have one—in the ballroom! On the second day I announced an early swim (in the drizzle) to wake everyone up, to a float about fifty yards away, where a tumbler of brandy awaited; after drinking it you swam back, if you could.

One of the main draws of the conference, in addition to our exciting and informative speakers, was the presence of the newly elected president of YPO. He worked the room for three days, and made a lot of friends, and a very good impression for the Empire Chapter. When the conference was over, he called a meeting with four or five key people. I was included because, he said, I'd just done such a bang-up job.

"What are we going to do about the Empire Chapter?" he asked.

It was a good question, as the chapter had declined seriously, a matter of great concern to the organization. Empire had been the very first chapter, Ray Hickock's chapter, and no one wanted to see it go under and its members absorbed by other chapters. We left the meeting with the problem unresolved, but I should have seen what was coming. In 1963 I was elected to my first office in the Empire chapter, and not too long after that I became its chairman.

I worked very hard, and made some important changes right away. For example, instead of meeting once a month as the chapter had been doing for years and years, I got the board to agree that we'd meet every quarter, and for three days at a time. I knew how big New York state was and how difficult it could be to get around, and I thought members would react positively to this idea, especially if we beefed up the content of the meetings with guest speakers such as Dick Beckhard and other attractions. I was right. The word quickly spread that our meetings were not just fun, they also had substance, and our membership reversed its decline and shot upward.

As a direct result of this success, I was appointed Northeast Area vice president in charge of all the chapters in that region for one year. In addition, I was talked into taking the post of education committee chairman for the national conference. That same year, a man named Al Self, whom I'd come to know very well, was elected president of YPO. Al asked me to take the vice president's job, which would have involved the overseeing of the annual conference. It would also mean, in all probability, that I would succeed him as president.

Taking the top job in YPO would have required me to give up my *real* job for a full year. And that was something I couldn't do. My father used to say, "Always ask yourself what your main job is. That's the one you do."

I declined the honor, and from then on I was strictly a participant in YPO. I was not given any new assignments, but by then that was just fine with me. I had already learned a tremendous amount. In fact, thanks to my YPO training, our sales conferences and other large and important meetings at The Raymond Corporation were held with far greater professionalism.

An important management tool I learned from Dick Beckhard and Bob Blake was Blake's Managerial Grid, a system in which you filled out an extensive questionnaire to determine where you stood—as a manager—on a scale of one to nine: a scale that indicated concern for production on one axis and for people on the other. My father would have scored 9,1 (favoring production), your basic autocrat; and I, who saw myself as the buffer between him and his other managers, would have scored 5,5. In fact, that was exactly what I did score when tested for the first time. I made it my goal, based on what I had gained at YPO seminars, to become a 9,9, the ultimate participative manager with concerns for both production and people.

In his book *Agent of Change,* Dick Beckhard gives an excellent definition/description of Blake's innovative discovery: "The grid was based on the theory that attitudes of managers in large part determined their behavior. The basic concept was that we all have some amount of concern for results and some amount of concern for people."

As an indication of how much value I came to place on the organizational development movement, we eventually "ran the managerial grid" on over 500 of our people. We came to know the process so well that we were soon teaching it ourselves. Everyone who went through the test clearly saw where he or she stood in relationship to the often opposing concepts of productivity and people. For the first time, managers and workers alike recognized what their priorities were. This self-awareness among the Raymond workforce translated directly into a better running, more productive company as we moved into the 1960s.

By 1965, my father was totally out of the managerial picture, but I couldn't help wondering how he might have viewed the grid and what it said about people, if someone as skilled and knowledgeable as Dick Beckhard or Bob Blake had been his guru, as they were mine. My father may have been an autocrat, but he was not small-minded, so I liked thinking he might well have come to see the program's merits and adopted its principles. Then again, he might have dismissed it outright.

In the larger world—that is, the world beyond Greene—word began getting around that something new was going on at The Raymond Corporation, something called "organizational development" which involved "T-groups." It wasn't long before the business press was knocking at our door. Around 1965 I got a call from a reporter from *Fortune,* requesting an interview. The result was an article that gave The Raymond Corporation, and its new CEO, some very nice publicity.

As the 1960s moved toward the 1970s, I did my level best to master the basics of participative or team management, and I believe I succeeded, for the most part. I recently asked Dick Beckhard for his objective assessment of how well I'd done. This is what he wrote:

> Because his father was so strong, George was very "influenceable" when he became president of The Raymond Corp. Fortunately for him the Young Presidents' Organization came along right about that time.
>
> I think that his great fear of growing up—and of course he knew he was going to run the company some day—was that he would have to run it the very same way his father did. And while he wasn't sure, early on, just how he wanted to run the company, the one thing he knew was that he didn't want to run it the way his father had.
>
> So being in YPO was a refuge for him and for all of those young people who were like him. YPO had seminars and education courses

and conferences. It was a wonderful thing for a young president. It not only made George, but it made many a young man. In fact, it was more than a refuge, it was a haven. But George wouldn't have been able to take advantage of any of this if he hadn't had that intense desire to learn—and to do things differently than his father.

I agree with Dick's assessment, mostly. I disagree with his use of the word "fear." I never feared that I would have to do things a certain way just because my father had. One of my favorite poems is "Mending Wall," by Robert Frost. A farmer is carrying stones to a boundary-marking wall, thinking to repair it after a long winter. The farmer's neighbor knows the farmer is only repairing the wall because his father had always done it. Like his father before him, the farmer says, as he places down a stone, "Good fences make good neighbors."

I'm all for good neighbors, walls or no walls; but I wasn't going to run The Raymond Corporation like my father out of loyalty to him or a tradition. I had stepped into his shoes, but I would make my own tracks.

In 1965, my father and I set up the Raymond Foundation with a start-up check of $150. Its purpose was to save on estate taxes at his death and to fund worthy causes in the community. It was originally organized with four trustees—in the beginning all of them family members (my parents, my sister, and me); later prominent local people from outside the family were added. Eventually, my three children would become trustees.

When my father died in 1967, the Foundation received an immediate one-million-dollar grant in Raymond Corporation stock. Under federal law, a charitable organization has to give away five percent of its assets on a yearly basis, and the Raymond Foundation lived up to its obligation.

One of its early successes was a community swimming pool in Greene. Residents wanted one badly, but when city officials heard it would cost $40,000 they said no way, too expensive. I said the Raymond Foundation would give 50 percent of the total cost if the community would give the other half. Several of us formed a group to raise the money. Donations poured in, and the Foundation contributed its share. Planning started immediately, and the pool opened the next summer.

For much of America the 1960s were a turbulent period. For Greene, New York, and those of us associated with The Raymond Corporation, it was relatively peaceful. I satisfied a lifelong childhood desire to have a saddle horse, and I bought one, a six-year-old Morgan gelding, which I boarded at a horse farm not far away. I had so much pleasure in owning and riding him that I soon bought a second horse, a mare, also a Morgan, which I bred to a Morgan stallion in a neighboring town. In 1962 Cynnie and I bought the property where we were to build our new house, 200 acres of woodland and pastureland, including a big old cow barn. I converted it into box stalls, and then I was on my way in the "Morgan business." I bred, trained, showed and sold Morgans for fifteen years. It was a rewarding (but costly) avocation.

I won't pretend we didn't have any political protests in Greene in the 1960s, because from time to time we did, but for the most part our community in the Southern Tier went on with everyday business without much fuss or bother.

The 1960s were the decade in which my children became teenagers, graduated from high school, and went off to college. That was a transformation that never ceased to amaze me. It seemed that one minute they were little kids and the next they were young adults. When they were children, I had spent a good bit of time with them and was one of the few young dads in our social circle who bottle-fed his kids (and even changed their diapers on occasion). I read to them regularly, played a lot of football on the lawn with the boys, rebuilt a five-horsepower outboard motor for our little wooden boat on the lake, and in general had a good deal of fun with my two sons and daughter—all this despite a schedule that kept me on the road half the time. My only "sacrifice" during this period was giving up golf.

As president of the Greene School Board, I personally handed my three children their high school diplomas—first Pete, then Steve, and finally Jean in 1971. It was a special moment for me, each time.

At the company, my energy remained focused on the goals that lay ahead. We were entering a period of great growth and increased competition, here and abroad, and I began implementing managerial changes—emphasis on teamwork—to meet those challenges and strengthen Raymond's position as the leader in the narrow-aisle lift truck industry.

5

On My Own
(At Last!)

hen Worthington Associates studied The Raymond Corporation in 1953, their final report contained three charts, each of which purported to describe the organizational structure of our company. Their point, which was certainly valid, was this: the way we said we were organized was not how we perceived we were to be organized, and it certainly was not how we were in fact organized. The charts (which appear on the following pages) were entitled, "Official Structure," "Perceived Structure," and "Actual Operating Structure."

I'm sorry to say Worthington's point was lost on my father; he saw nothing wrong with our structure, on paper or in reality. But it was not lost on me. I vowed that when I took over, I would do my best to make sure everyone in the company had a clear understanding of how The Raymond Corporation was structured, where the lines of force ran, and who was answerable to whom. Most important, I wanted everyone to understand that we were all on the same team.

There's a common belief that you can't change your personality, but that was exactly what I was attempting to do when I took over as CEO in 1959. Realizing from Bob Blake's "managerial grid" that I was a "5,5," or compromise manager, I made a purposeful, dedicated effort to change my management style and become a "9,9,"

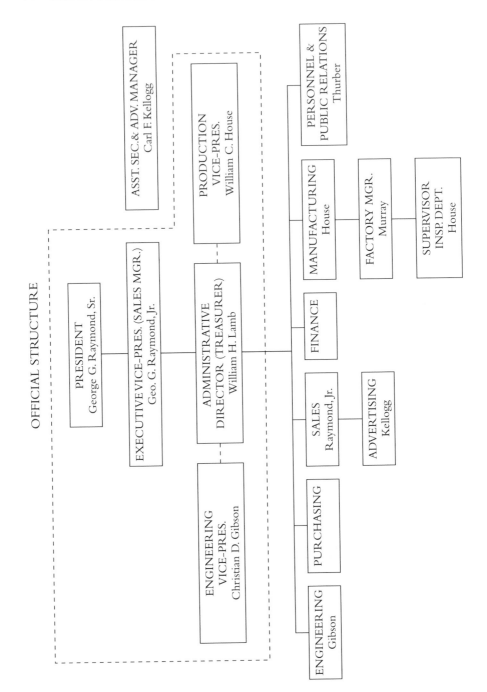

OFFICIAL STRUCTURE

PRESIDENT
George G. Raymond, Sr.

EXECUTIVE VICE-PRES. (SALES MGR.)
Geo. G. Raymond, Jr.

ASST. SEC. & ADV. MANAGER
Carl F. Kellogg

ADMINISTRATIVE
DIRECTOR (TREASURER)
William H. Lamb

PRODUCTION
VICE-PRES.
William C. House

ENGINEERING
VICE-PRES.
Christian D. Gibson

ENGINEERING
Gibson

PURCHASING

SALES
Raymond, Jr.

ADVERTISING
Kellogg

FINANCE

MANUFACTURING
House

FACTORY MGR.
Murray

SUPERVISOR
INSP. DEPT.
House

PERSONNEL &
PUBLIC RELATIONS
Thurber

PERCEIVED STRUCTURE

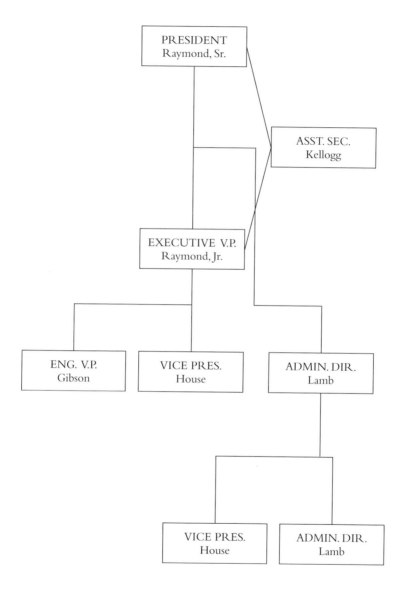

ACTUAL OPERATING STRUCTURE
("RADIAL")

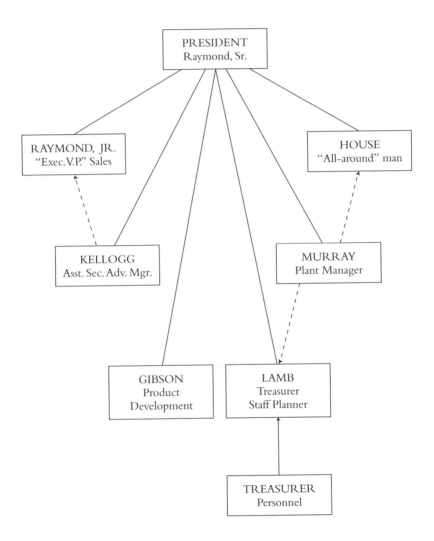

the ultimate participative manager with high concerns for both production and people.

The T-groups and the managerial grid, and all the teaching and coaching of Dick Beckhard and Bob Blake, were the vehicles of my transformation, my liberation from the powerful influence of my father and his way of running a company. But it all started with the Worthington report in 1953. For me, the report validated the psychological approach to business management—the idea that an understanding of how people act as people has a direct relationship to how people act in business. Today that seems obvious, but back then it was a new idea.

Consider this, from Alfred J. Marrow's *Behind the Executive Mask:*

> Until the second world war the behavioral sciences showed little interest in the problems of business management. Insofar as they dealt with the subject at all, psychologists were concerned primarily with production workers. Little research was directed at the problems or the techniques of management. In recent years, however, many systematic inquiries have been made about the factors that contribute to the successful management of people. Much research has been directed to the relationship between managerial approach, employee productivity, and job satisfaction. As a result, there is much less distrust between the managers of American business and the practitioners of modern psychology. Behavioral scientists and industrial leaders now know that they have much to learn from one another.

What's so impressive about that particular statement is that Dr. Marrow wrote it in the early 1960s. At 140 pages, his book is a slim volume, but the author has packed more information into each page than many books on management contain in each chapter. Here's an example that caught me up short: "The average manager's answer to the question of who is to be changed is that it is the workers or his boss. He doesn't think of changing himself." One of the reasons I had the success I eventually had with The Raymond Corporation is that I *did* think of changing myself, and worked long and hard to do it.

A couple of things explain why I found this little book so relevant to the task I had set for myself and the company I was now running. For one thing, Al Marrow was no mere academic theoretician. Here's what the president of the American Management Association, Lawrence Appley, had to say in his foreword to Marrow's work.

> There are few people as well equipped as Alfred J. Marrow to write this kind of book—a book that applies the findings and methods of the human sciences to the art of getting things done through people.... His work serves as a bridge linking scientific knowledge of human behavior and the economic objectives of the company.... The sensitivity training of which Dr. Marrow writes so persuasively is a tool of growing importance in helping managers win the cooperation of the people they work with and through. More often than not this is a painful process, forcing the manager to break ingrained patterns of behavior and form new ones; yet a typical executive has called it, "the most challenging and beneficial experience of my entire business career."

AMA president Appley wasn't quoting me, but he could have been, for that is exactly the way I would have described my experiences with T-groups, organizational development, and the human development movement in general.

My feelings about Marrow were summarized by Warren G. Bennis, a professor of industrial management at MIT, in his introduction to Marrow's "little book."

> The manager can no longer be construed narrowly as a manager of a technological-financial system. He must be seen as the center of a highly complex and dynamic human network where he negotiates, transacts, and exchanges with a host of factors, external and internal, human and institutional.... If an enterprise is to succeed, the manager must develop keen eyes and ears for the human forces surrounding him upon whose resources the enterprise stands or falls. In short, the manager must develop interpersonal competence, an ability that is becoming less a luxury than a necessity in a time when human motivation is so crucial to success....

It's not hard to see why this book appealed to me so strongly. The idea of using Marrow's emerging knowledge—briefly stated, how one functions as a person is key to understanding how one can function better as a manager—was at the very heart of what I was trying to learn and then instill in managers and workers alike at Raymond. Admittedly, these concepts were foreign to my father's way of doing business; but for me they were, quite simply, what I was all about.

I was so impressed with Dick Beckhard and his work that I asked him to become a consultant to The Raymond Corporation and to teach us the tenets of the human potential movement. Phrasing it that way was my first mistake. As Dick immediately pointed out, the beauty of the movement was that it relied on self-instruction as the road to self-knowledge.

In his book, Marrow says:

> Sensitivity training is often called laboratory training because it encourages the individual to examine his own behavior and to experiment with new ways of relating to others. The subjects of the experiment are also the participants. The training laboratory is the special environment in which they learn new things about themselves. The participant is in the unique position of being at the same time both the experimenter and the subject of the experiment.

We called on Bob Blake to come to Greene and give us our first training in the understanding and use of the managerial grid. By answering a list of skillfully crafted questions, a person could determine where he or she stood along two axes: in one focusing on "concern for production" and in the other focusing on "concern for people." A score of 9,1 (favoring production) made you an "authoritarian"; a score of 1,9 (favoring people) marked you "country club." If you came in a 1,1 it positioned you in the "Oh, who gives a damn anyway?" category, and if you were 5,5 you were a compromise manager. The "team manager, or participative manager," would score a 9,9.

The day came for a dress rehearsal. Blake sent his assistant, an enthusiastic young man with a well-trimmed beard, to see if we were ready to go ahead with the grid-training program in the company. Trouble was, we hadn't prepared for the visit; there was a lot for us to learn and study and we just hadn't got around to it. After all, we had an expert coming in from out of town. Why should we bother? The end result was, we fell on our faces. We wanted the expert to come in and call the shots, take us by the hand. Well, it doesn't work that way.

Modern management is a two-way street, with a continuous back-and-forth flow, but after Blake's assistant left I saw that we were still stuck on the one-way street of tradition and habit. To change would require outside experts, but what it was really going to take, on our part, was work. Hard, dedicated work. We all know personal habits are hard to break. Often, we don't even bother trying. Changing the "habits" of a company, I was to find out, was really more a Herculean task than a managerial undertaking.

One setback wasn't going to make me scrap my initiative, however. I've always been one to learn from mistakes and failures, and when we did a repeat session, two months later, without any outside assistance, we were prepared.

As it developed, when we did the second group, we didn't have enough participants from management, so we added three people from manufacturing. I didn't tell anybody at the time, but I'd wondered from the beginning if the idea of the managerial grid could also be used on the manufacturing floor and in the offices. One afternoon, about halfway through the program, I was walking down the hallway when one of the participants from manufacturing, a welder named Sal Vitone, was hurrying along in the opposite direction and almost knocked me over.

"Sorry, George," he said, not stopping. "Got to get back to my group. This is the greatest thing I've ever done!" Sal happened to be one of the most vocal pro-union guys in the entire company, but his experience with the managerial grid gave him a whole new perspective on the company and his role in it.

In the middle of that week, union organizers showed up at the plant and began handing out leaflets. On Friday, Sal and another pro-union plant worker named Rudy who had been in the same grid session, went to the office of the vice-president of manufacturing, independently. As Jim Harty told me later that same day, "Vitone said he was really impressed with this grid thing. He said, 'If you guys are trying this hard to change the company, then I'll do everything I can to defeat the union.' Rudy seconded him chapter and verse."

The next time the option of union membership came up for a vote, it was defeated by a three to one margin. Who needed a union when workers and managers were all part of the same team?

It cost us a pretty penny to include manufacturing and office personnel in the behavioral science testing and group sessions at Raymond. When workers are away from their workstations, they obviously aren't doing any productive work on the floor or at a desk; plus, training and group days always ran well past five o'clock, and we paid our people time and a half for those extra hours. But this was no time for shortsighted economics. To make money you have to spend money; those words were never truer than they were for Raymond during that period. Anything we spent in self-awareness training we soon made up in increased productivity, and we had a workforce of people who believed in their product, their company, but most importantly themselves.

I'll never forget an experience I had in the mid-1960s when we were testing a new welding fixture, or jig, for the first time. When I walked up to the group of men surrounding the jig, I saw from the looks on their faces that something was wrong; for some reason the steel parts weren't fitting the way they were supposed to. In short, there was a problem. There were ten engineers around the jig, and one welder standing off to the side. The engineers were scratching their heads.

I knew Les, the welder, very well, so I spoke to him first and asked him if he knew what the trouble was.

"Sure," he replied.

"Can you fix it?"

"No problem. Take me two minutes."

Then I walked over to the engineers and asked them how they were doing, and they told me they couldn't figure out what was wrong with the jig.

"Who knows the most about it?" I asked.

"We do," one of them answered. "We designed it."

"Well," I said, "Les over there told me he knows what's wrong. Why don't you bring him in and see what he says."

They did, and soon the parts were fitting perfectly. Some people think that just because they have a college degree they're smarter than someone who doesn't, someone who only knows his trade. That's a dangerous, limiting way of thinking. Les had been one of the first people in manufacturing to sign up for managerial grid training, and I know he got a lot more out of it than quite a few of my managers.

Another pitfall we had to experience before "getting it right" was our tendency to rely too heavily on our guru. Dick Beckhard finally broke us of that habit in a very dramatic fashion.

I had worked out a consulting arrangement with Dick whereby he gave us three days every quarter. He would arrive in Greene, get us started on a new way of thinking, of looking at ourselves and the company; and when he left he would instruct us to keep the ball rolling on our own. Well, for quite a while in the first year or two, whenever he would leave we'd go right back to our old behavioral patterns instead of putting what we'd just learned to good use. He said we were the best diagnosticians—and the worst executors—he'd ever worked with.

On his fifth visit to Greene, Dick, who had been increasingly tough on us with each visit, lowered the boom. We still hadn't done our strategic planning, hoping, perhaps unconsciously, that he would do it for us, even though we knew he couldn't; for him to help us directly went against the very concept of the program. So this time when he arrived on a Sunday night, planning to stay until Wednesday afternoon as usual, and saw that once again we hadn't done our homework, he simply looked me in the eye and said, "You're supposed to be doing this yourselves. Stop thinking of me as a crutch! I'm leaving, I'll see you in three months. And by the way, I'm charging you the full three-day fee."

And with that, off he went. It was a short session but an effective one. From then on we didn't rely on anyone but ourselves. When Dick returned the following quarter, he told us, after our first session together that The Raymond Corporation had finally broken its ties with old-school managerial concepts. We were on our way to becoming a "modern American company."

"And don't be surprised," he added, "if you see your profits soar."

And soar they did. For my first five years as head of the company, our annual revenues had hovered around the $5 million dollar mark. But in the mid-1960s, when I began implementing what I'd learned in the organizational development movement, revenues began climbing. By the early 1970s they had reached $35–$40 million per year.

I always remembered what Dick had said that day: "Don't be surprised..."

I wasn't. I was delighted.

Our work was paying off.

6

A Whole New
Ball Game

When Dick Beckhard started consulting with The Raymond Corporation in the early 1960s, he helped us identify one of our biggest problems: a breakdown in communications. In fact, we weren't communicating at all! I'd begun to spread the word that Raymond was going to become a different type of organization, one with problem-centered decision making and individual freedom in managing. That was what I said, but it was not what people heard; or, if they heard, they didn't believe what I'd said.

To be more specific, early on in my tenure as president, as part of my overall plan to shift the decision-making authority closer to the problem, I asked my design chiefs to look into a new product I'd heard about in England, a counter-balanced electric forklift truck. Wanting to fill out Raymond's line of material-handling vehicles—we made chiefly a narrow-aisle truck that "straddled" a pallet and didn't need counter-balancing—I gave my managers the assignment of deciding whether the company should buy the rights to manufacture the truck in the United States. A counter-balanced vehicle might open new markets for us. When they reported back to me that it looked like an excellent deal, I went ahead with it. We manufactured several vehicles but the line didn't take hold, and the whole project flopped to the tune of half a million dollars.

It took me a good while to find out what had happened: Despite my instructions that Raymond managers do an objective analysis of the truck, they thought I'd already made up my mind to manufacture and sell it. As a result, they didn't tell me their real opinion: the truck didn't meet company standards and would have to be totally redesigned. My managers told me what they thought I wanted to hear, not what their expert opinion told them I should hear. Why? Because managers at Raymond didn't dare make judgments or think for themselves. Thinking was done by the man at the top.

In a word, middle and lower management weren't absorbing top management's ideas for change; they continued to do things the old way because it had become so ingrained.

With Dick Beckhard's help, I moved to rectify the situation by meeting with all of my upper-level managers at a three-day conference at the American Management Association's new facility in Hamilton, New York. By this time almost everyone in the company had become familiar with the Managerial Grid. Armed with the factual data from the test materials, I asked the managers to evaluate my managerial style and performance. Boy, did I get an earful! I learned that my words and actions weren't coming across as I intended. That is, what I saw myself to be saying wasn't necessarily what my managers were hearing. They were interpreting my words instead of taking what I said at face value. In simplest terms, they weren't believing me.

After a lengthy go-around at the AMA facility, we ironed out the problem. We really started talking—about our goals as a company, where we wanted to see Raymond in five years, where we saw ourselves in five years. When the conference ended, my vice-president of manufacturing, Don Colson, came up to me and said, "George, in all the different companies I've worked for, I've never seen anything like this. Discussing issues that matter to *all* of us? It's a first!"

Excited by the success of the Hamilton conference, I huddled with Dick and my top people, wanting to implement throughout the company the "laboratory approach" that had just worked so effectively in the smaller group. We utilized a number of different teaching devices, from T-groups, to the Grid, to team-building labs conducted in-house. I told every manager that I thought he should make use of one or more of these techniques, but I did not insist on it. The whole idea was to get people together to talk, to express themselves openly and honestly. It was my fervent hope that no Raymond employee would be afraid, from now on, to say what he or she thought.

With each new step, I became more and more confident that the management style of George Raymond Jr. was the right one for the company as we entered the "modern era."

I didn't need an endorsement to prove that organizational development—OD—was working for us, because I knew it was. Still, endorsements poured in, and one stands out in my mind. During one of our grid-lab sessions, a production worker stopped me at the break and said, "You know what I've just come to realize, George? Even if you do your job well, it won't mean anything if I don't do *my* job well."

"Dan," I replied, "you've just put into a nutshell what this is all about."

Unsolicited testimonials are great, but so is a solid bottom line. Here are some hard facts: in the first five years of the OD movement, our sales rose from $7.6 million to $23 million, with net income going from $520,000 to $1.2 million, and earnings per share from 72 cents to $1.31. Our growth rate over that same period was 10 to 15 percent higher than that of the material-handling industry as a whole. All during that period of steady growth, I heard Dick Beckhard's words in my head, "Don't be surprised if..."

In the late 1960s, Dick Thurber, our head of personnel, commented about our program in *Fortune* magazine: "We've just begun to realize what it means to unleash the human resources potential in this company," he said. "Just as individuals grow from dependent children to self-responsible adults, an organization should grow to the point that it can stand on its own two feet and function as a mature entity."

About that time a foreman in the plant was demoted for "incompetence," as I heard it, and middle management tried to promote someone from within the company. When they couldn't find anyone, they posted the job on the outside and even used a recruiter, all to no avail. As part of our new protocol at Raymond, the managers went back inside and asked the men in the demoted foreman's department to suggest names of possible candidates, and the only name they came up with was the demoted foreman's.

They said that Joe had actually known his job and done it well. There had been a misunderstanding between him and his boss, who had demoted him. The men suggested that management rethink the demotion and give the foreman his old job back. The managers checked this out, learned that the men were right, and reinstated the foreman. Then they suggested a meeting between the two men. They dealt with the issues in a straightforward manner and resolved their differences. As a result, that department became one of the most productive in the company.

In 1969, we received praise for our new managerial philosophy from the National Industrial Conference Board, a prestigious fifty-year-old non-profit business research outfit made up of 4,000 member organizations worldwide. Part of its "Studies in Personnel Policy" series, *Behavioral Science: Concepts and Management Application,* featured case study profiles of ten companies. We found ourselves among the likes of such brand names as American Airlines, Armstrong Cork, Corning Glass, The Hotel Corporation of America, Texas Instruments, and TRW.

After informing its readers where we were headquartered and that we manufactured material-handling equipment, that our sales in 1967 were $23 million and our employees numbered 850, the article began by quoting what it called an old management proverb. "Any company—regardless of its size—is pretty much the length and breadth of the man at the top." It then went on to say:

> Take the case of a young man who accedes to the presidency in a family-owned corporation that was previously run by his father. He inherits an organization that is probably the "length and breadth of the man at the top." He is then faced with deciding between living with the organization, its value systems, and its organizational culture (which has probably existed for a long time), or devising a way to generate change in the organization that will be conducive to further growth.
>
> The second alternative is often chosen because of the ever-accelerating pace of change in the external environment and the increased competition in the market place that the organization must come to grips with.
>
> This was the problem that George G. Raymond Jr. found himself confronted with when, in 1953, he succeeded his father as president of The Raymond Corporation, and the senior Raymond remained chairman of the board. Working in various capacities under his father, he had obtained, and contributed to, some growth in the company; but as president he was concerned about the long-range prospects for the company's survival in an industry dominated by giants.
>
> The problem George Raymond Jr. faced was how to find a way to utilize human resources so that the employees—in production, design, manufacturing, and sales—would outproduce the giants. He reports that he tried three different approaches with varying degrees of success.

Using the labels affixed by the case study's author, those three approaches were: benevolent dictatorship, scientific management, and team management. In actuality, I hadn't tried the first approach myself: "strong authoritarianism of the carrot-and-stick variety tempered by family paternalism" was my father's trademark.

True, the company had grown dramatically since 1950, with profits paralleling this growth. But I was concerned that we had no firm base from which to continue growing. Our managers had great responsibility but absolutely no authority! I remember my father's reaction when I told him that I wanted to take our top executives away from the plant for a few days of "long-range planning." He said, "What for? Waste of good man hours!"

Regardless of the negative spin he had put on the idea, my managers and I went to the Skytop Lodge in the Poconos for three days of intense discussion. We batted around every aspect of business and management. When we returned to the plant Monday morning, my father was quick to ask me what we'd done.

"We did a lot of talking," I said.

"You could've talked here."

"It was important to get away."

He threw me one of his patented skeptical looks. "What did you decide?"

"To double sales and profits every five years."

"George, it's a lot harder to go from five million to ten million than it is to go from one million to two!"

I showed him the current copy of *Time* magazine with a picture of Tom Watson Jr. of IBM on the cover, and the statement, "IBM to double in five years."

My father, a great admirer of Watson and his company, said, "Well, good luck."

He was typical of the managers of his generation, working hard and making sure everyone else did, too. He would build up someone's self-image by asking his or her opinion on an issue, then promptly ignore or forget what that person had said and do what he had intended to do in the first place. That problem existed for a long time in The Raymond Corporation, whether my father was there in person, or only in spirit.

The article in "Studies in Personnel Policy" continued:

George Raymond Jr. observed that the "benevolent dictatorship" climate he inherited was glaringly apparent in several ways. For example, from the first day when he became president, he had to make the final decisions on every issue of any importance in every area of the company. Furthermore, there were no written policies or operating guidelines; rather managers had nothing to follow except past practices—if they were remembered.

Moving away from the "autocratic paternalism" of his father, George Raymond Jr. decided to try a second approach to managing, the approach he called "scientific" management—a style that is often identified with managing through systems and procedures. For the first time in the history of the company, some policies, procedures, and practices were defined in writing. Responsibilities were specifically spelled out, along with corresponding authority and accountability. George Raymond Jr. felt that this move helped improve the organization because official channels of communication were delineated, and managers had, in writing, what was expected of them. But, he reported, the managers were still doing everything the old way. In other words, he found no real evidence of change in the basic fabric or climate of the organization.

Much as I may have differed with my father's way of running a company, I never openly criticized it while he was in charge. But I have to say that decades of his "benevolent autocracy" made it hard to introduce, much less effect, change—though sixteen years after taking the helm I had made considerable progress.

Near the end of the National Industrial Conference Board's case study, the author wrote:

These team-building sessions aren't just another exercise to build cohesiveness within the organization generally, though this is one thing the company hopes to accomplish through them. Rather, Raymond tries to build teams to do special projects. The organization chart of The Raymond Corporation resembles those of most other companies and it is structured along traditional lines. But the company is increasingly using interdepartmental task force teams that cut across organizational boundaries and encompass people at all levels of the organization. The company conceptualizes these "working family teams" as "floating task groups" that are superimposed on its traditional (pyramid) structure. That is, each member remains in his allocated spot to perform his usual duty, while he also belongs to the task group that functions as a temporary system which may exist for as short as a week or for as long as three years, until the project is completed.

The president insists that these task groups are not part of the project management style of managing. "A project manager," he explains, "functions as a coordinator and boss; whereas, in a floating task group the decisions that must be made, plus the corresponding responsibility and accountability for them, change from one time to another as the project progresses. And the leadership constantly shifts from one person to another, depending upon who has expertise in dealing with a particular problem." Since the job of the floating task group is to interact with each other and since each group is responsible for the efforts of its members, accountability for the success or failure of the project is on a group basis too.

George Raymond Jr. believes that the company's period of experimenting and testing behavioral science applications is over. He views the company as totally committed to the behavioral science approach to managing, and he anticipates further involvement with behavioral science applications in the future on a systematically planned basis. For this reason the company feels that it needs its own resident professional behavioral scientist to advise and direct future OD efforts, and plans to add one to the staff on a full-time permanent basis. The efforts of the behavioral scientist will be fully integrated with all other functions of the company's operations.

In summing up, George Raymond Jr. says, "I think we have reached the point of information and experience where we can now begin to develop in-house a five-year plan for development of human resources, just as we now plan and forecast our production output and marketing strategies. This is because we have begun to produce an organization that is attuned to change, and we now have people in the company with expertise in managing human resources, just as a finance man of any company has expertise in planning and budgeting financial assets, both now and in the future. We are becoming capable of doing this ourselves without dependence on consultants or canned programs. Organization development should be carefully geared to suit the needs of the organization it serves. All organizations are different because the people that compose them are different."

A lingering effect of my father's long-time presence was that managers and workers on all levels were still hesitant, if not afraid, to walk into the executive wing, even when my father was away from the plant, spending his winters in Florida. All things considered, it shouldn't have been that surprising. After all, here was a man who had decreed back when the company was just getting started that all employees had to live in Greene. They couldn't live in Binghamton or any of the little nearby towns. Why? Because when there was a bad snow (and we had at least three big storms each winter), employees could all still get to work—on foot.

I remember one time we had a brutal ice storm during the night, and in my office early the next morning I decided that the only smart thing to do was close the plant for the day. Just as I'd made that decision, I looked out my window and saw people walking toward the main entrance ten and twenty at a time. Every single Raymond employee got to work that day, including a turret-lathe operator named Walter, whose truck slid off the road into a ditch. He left it there and walked the rest of the way, some seven miles!

Once I saw the extent of the fear my father had created in his employees, I made a number of changes in the way certain things were done in the company. The commemorative "Service Pin" ceremony is an example. Starting in 1947, whenever an employee hit a particular milepost—five years, ten, fifteen and so on—my father would call that employee into his office and make a little ceremony, complete with photographer, of the event. Thinking the workers loved the whole thing as much as my father obviously did, I carried on the tradition. But I'd only made a few presentations when my long-time secretary clued me in and told me that, in truth, the employees hated the ceremony because it made them so nervous. Okay, I said; and from then on I awarded the pin to employees at their workplace in the office or factory. They got to hear their coworkers' applause, they still had their picture taken and put in the company newsletter; but best of all they escaped the ordeal of having to go into the "president's office." All in all, this was a big improvement, the kind of thing a behavioral scientist could have pointed out to my father decades earlier. Whether he would have listened is another matter.

One of the great benefits of bringing organizational development and the team concept of management to Raymond was that we lost so few people under the new "regime." Of the 282 people who trained to any extent with the Grid, 259 were still with Raymond five years after indoctrination into the program. Of those 259, 19 were promoted to group leader or specialist positions, 18 were promoted to managerial jobs, 6 who were already managers were promoted to even higher positions, and 57 others were promoted or "transferred up." In anyone's book, it was an impressive record.

During virtually every visit Dick Beckhard made to Greene in those years, Cynnie and I would invite him to have dinner with us. And what times they were! Almost before we knew it, he would be turning our evening meal into a mini encounter-group. To my surprise, the kids loved it, especially Pete, who was about 16 when this began. With Dick Beckhard, anything was fair game in a session, and Pete thoroughly enjoyed the opportunities to go at it with his father.

It became obvious to me about then that Pete and I did not see eye to eye on most things. Like me, he made the varsity football team at Greene High, but unlike me he displayed a reluctance to mix it up. He was taller than I had been and a little heavier, so it wasn't that he lacked size. I remember watching one play from the sidelines and wondering why he didn't charge in and help tackle the ball carrier.

The next time he came off the field, I asked him, and he surprised me by saying, "I didn't want to hurt the kid." That attitude persisted for over a year until an opposing player threw a vicious block at him. When Pete got up he was mad, clear through, and he made every tackle after that.

But his attitude toward me didn't change, and we continued marching to different drummers. Granted, it was a different era, a time of anti-establishment protest; by itself, that could have been the reason we didn't see eye to eye. Still, I couldn't help remembering that when I was his age I did everything my father asked, pretty much without questioning it. Pete questioned almost everything I said. There was no badness in him; it was just that he looked at life from a different perspective. While I had dreamed of following in my father's footsteps, that concept never entered my son's mind.

Pete enjoyed physical work and the great outdoors. He often said he loved skiing so much that he wouldn't mind living in a tent at the bottom of the mountain and eating nothing but granola! Another one of his favorite sayings was that if he was going to be a ditch-digger—which he actually was for a while—he would damn well be the best ditch-digger in town. One job he had was with a ready-mix concrete company in Greene. His boss, who was a friend of mine and had known the family for years, asked him why he was breaking his back, instead of sitting behind a Raymond company desk. Pete said, "I have to prove myself to myself."

"Then why don't you give up the company stock your grandfather left you?"

Pete replied that he wasn't ready to go that far.

When he was a senior at Greene High he decided he wanted to become a Green Beret and fight in Vietnam. Having been in World War II, I knew how dangerous warfare was, and Pete's volunteering for front-line duty made little sense to me. We went round and round on that one. Fortunately, he cooled on the idea and did not enlist.

After high school, Pete went to Claremont College in California—about as far away from home as he could get. He made it through his first year when he decided toss college aside and marry his high school sweetheart Sue Gibson, the daughter of Raymond's chief engineer. We were not delighted; Pete was nineteen.

He left Claremont College and took a job at General Electric in Binghamton as a material handler—an entry level job in a factory. With a wife, and a child on the way, he soon realized he wouldn't be able to support his family on the low pay. He went back to school, first at Broome Tech in Binghamton, then at Arizona State at Tempe, where he showed everyone he meant business by earning a 4.0 grade-point average while working nights to support his family. Sadly, his marriage broke up in 1979 as he was nearing graduation, and he never finished the few credits he needed for his diploma. Pete left Tempe and, quite literally, disappeared. No one heard from him for a month and a half.

He finally surfaced in California, where he had tramped up and down the state in an effort to come to terms with his failed marriage. He loved his very young children, Todd and Noel, and having his family disintegrate was a crushing blow. Younger brother Steve, who had just finished a five-year stint in the Air Force and was studying at SUNY Binghamton for his graduate degree in business administration, flew out to the Coast to drive back with him across the country. Instead of heading for Greene, however, they drove to Dick Beckhard's place in Maine.

What was discussed, I won't pretend to know, but having a heart-to-heart with Dick couldn't have hurt. A few days later, both sons pulled into Greene. Steve returned to his studies in Binghamton, and Pete—perhaps because of his visit with Dick—started working for The Raymond Corporation. Not in a managerial capacity but on the assembly floor. Nonetheless, it was a step, and he was excellent at what he did, such as spotting problems—like the need for better ventilation in the paint shop. But he would never bring his ideas to my attention at the plant, preferring to wait until those occasions when he'd have dinner with his mother and me at the house. I tried to get him to come to my office with these suggestions, but he wouldn't do it.

Meanwhile, Steve was coming into his own. Even when he was a boy, Dick Beckhard saw him as a "leader." He had graduated with honors from Cornell's School of Industrial Engineering, then had joined the Air Force and done what his father had so dearly wanted to do: he became a pilot! He had flown huge jet tankers for in-flight fueling of fighter planes, an operation that took great concentration and skill; the fighter pilots had to trust you, and you had to trust them.

Now, a civilian again, Steve was finishing the spring semester at Binghamton. In June he came to the company as assistant to the sales manager, who soon urged him—not wanting to miss Steve's outstanding contributions to the sales force—to pursue his advanced degree at night. Steve took his advice, and in another year and a half had his MBA. Soon afterward he became sales manager at Raymond when that position opened up.

Pete continued in the company, in marketing, and was doing a good job. He had met a new woman, and before long they were talking about marriage. Karen was an expediter in purchasing, an attractive and intelligent woman. I was pleased and happy for them both and liked thinking that Pete was finding himself, at last; but I was soon to learn that he really hadn't changed at all. He was still recalcitrant Pete. At the altar during the rehearsal, the Rev. David Robinson, who was officiating, turned to my son and said, "Repeat after me. I, George—"

"I'm Pete!"

Everyone was stunned. I could hardly believe what I'd just heard. "That might be your nickname," Father Robinson said, "but in this church, for your wedding vows, you're George."

Under duress he said, "I, George—"

Since his earliest days Pete had distanced himself from me, and he was still doing it—even to the extent of denying his name was "George" before the eyes of God! I took a painful breath, wondering where I had failed him as a father. Perhaps, when he was growing up, I had spent too much time at the office, on the road, at school board meetings and Rotary functions. To do it any differently wouldn't have been me, but I had lost a son along the way, and I didn't see how, at this point, I would ever gain him back. I found myself reflecting on a photograph dating back exactly thirty years, and my father's caption: "Three generations—George Sr., George Jr., and George III. In due time George III is scheduled to carry on the future efforts of the company."

Images from a Life

LYON IR

The roughshod Lyon Iron Works manufactures
"almost anything a farmer or individual might
need" when George Raymond, Sr. buys it in
1922 for $6,000 with nothing down. It soldiers
on and twenty years later he renames it the Lyon-
Raymond Corporation, then in 1949 he names it
anew: The Raymond Corporation with his son
and v.p. George, Jr. pointing the way (inset).
The new sign declares the family firm's forte:
material handling equipment—forklifts, hand
trucks, conveyors and such—stock in trade that
will raise the company's worth to $353 million.

OFFICE

ADAMS

George Jr. lives an All-American boyhood in an All-American town, Greene, New York, graduating from Greene High School in 1939—here's his yearbook picture—both a football star and honor student. That fall he enters Cornell, his father's alma mater, just as Hitler invades Poland to ignite World War II. The war will interrupt his college career, permanently; his father needs him to come home to work for the family factory.

Knowing he will soon be in uniform, George marries his college sweetheart, Cynthia Spencer, in 1942. He tries to enlist in the Army Air Corps but gets drafted into the regular army and joins the 740th Anti-Aircraft Battalion. He stands right under the company colors when Company D's photograph is taken—a stand-out as usual. He makes sergeant, and his unit sees action in the Battle of the Bulge with General George Patton's Third Army.

In 1945 his parents (opposite) relish his safe return, and George Sr. starts to groom his son and heir to take over the family firm—some day. He steps aside in 1953 and names George Jr. president of The Raymond Corporation.

Within three years George is elected to the select Young President's Organization, and shines at its convention with Cynnie at his side (Above). By now they have three children, George III (called Pete), Steve and Jean, the baby.

George Sr. kicked himself upstairs, but still holds the purse strings and controls the firm. Still, George Jr. orders innovations in management methods and a new line of machines. Having weathered the depression and war, The Raymond Corporation is a major force in the vicinity and Greene's biggest employer.

MAY 28, 1956

*S*TEEL
The Metalworking Weekly

A PENTON PUBLICATION

Integrated Handling . . .

"It means control at the management, policy-making level" . . . page 106

George G. Raymond Jr., President Material Handling Institute Inc..

▶ **Bulk Handling in Steelmaking** . . page 114

▶ **Guide to the Handling Show** . . . page 129

CONTENTS — PAGE 5

MATERIAL HANDLING ISSUE

By 1956, George Jr. is a big man in business, even a trade magazine cover boy.

OVERLEAF: President also of the Material Handling Institute, he wields the scissors at a ribbon-cutting and receives a salute from another president, Dwight Eisenhower, again with Cynnie beside him.

WESTERN UNION

1290

W. P. MARSHALL, PRESIDENT

CLASS OF SERVICE		SYMBOLS
This is a full-rate Telegram or Cablegram unless its deferred character is indicated by a suitable symbol above or preceding the address.		DL=Day Letter
		NL=Night Letter
		LT=Int'l Letter Telegram
		VLT=Int'l Victory Ltr.

The filing time shown in the date line on telegrams and day letters is STANDARD TIME at point of origin. Time of receipt is STANDARD TIME at point of destination

PA196 AB699

A WA567 LONG GOVT NL PD=THE WHITE HOUSE WASHINGTON DC=
GEORGE G RAYMOND JR, PRESIDENT=
    THE MATERIAL HANDLING INSTITUTE INC ONE GATEWAY CENTER
PGH=

PLEASE EXTEND MY GREETINGS TO MEMBERS OF THE MATERIAL
HANDLING INSTITUTE AND VISITORS ATTENDING YOUR EXPOSITION
IN CLEVELAND.
    GREAT STRIDES HAVE BEEN TAKEN BY THE MATERIAL
HANDLING INDUSTRY IN DEVELOPING SPEEDY MECHANICAL METHODS
TO ASSIST WORKERS IN MOVING HEAVY BURDENS. INCREASED
EFFICIENCY IN THE HANDLING OF MATERIALS MAKES A VALUABLE
CONTRIBUTION TO DEFENSE AND INDUSTRIAL PROGRESS.
    ALL OF YOU HAVE MY BEST WISHES FOR A SUCCESSFUL
EXPOSITION=
    DWIGHT D EISENHOWER=.

The family firm thrives with George at the helm, at first thanks most to his decision to develop a new product, the narrow-aisle forklift truck. It revolutionizes material-handling and warehousing, letting a warehouse use 60 percent of its space for storage and 40 percent for aisles—the reverse of previous numbers. When state legislators visit the plant to see the little work-horse, George gives them a guided tour (inset).

Tragedy strikes: Cynnie is murdered by a deranged Vietnam vet, and George, his world turned upsidedown, vows to start over. Old friends introduce him to the smart and beautiful Robin Ylvisaker (right), a Chicago photographer. They are married on October 14, 1978, with his children, now grown (below) in attendance: Steve (left), Pete and Jean.

A supremely happy couple, Robin and George find new places to see and new causes to pursue. Leaving Greene, soon they make homes in Nantucket and Naples, Florida. They fund efforts to study and strengthen America's family firms, the most common form of business in the land. Finally George gets a college degree: an honorary doctorate from Alfred University.

OVERLEAF:
George commissioned a matched pair of portraits of his parents, George Gamble Raymond, Sr. and Madeleine Crombie Raymond, for The Raymond Corporation lobby. Now they hang in the public library in their old home town.

George retires—after a fashion—in 1987 (left),
surrounded by his extended family: Karen
Raymond (Pete's wife), Maxine Raymond
(Steve's wife), Steve, Robin, her daughter Laurie,
Pete, and Larry Keeley (husband of Robin's
daughter Beth who is behind camera).

At his retirement banquet George
celebrates passing the torch with his
friend and advisor, Dick Beckhard
(center), and Ross Colquoun, his hand-
picked successor at The Raymond
Corporation. Colquoun soon becomes
his adversary in a bitter battle over the
value and destiny of the old family
firm.

The battle won—the family firm is sold
to a conglomerate for $33 a share—
George and Robin radiate the joy of
their twentieth wedding anniversary.
He opens an investment firm. They
establish an institute and endow profes-
sorial chairs—in family business—at
Alfred University's School of Business.
Life is good, life is long—together.

7

The Board and I

The first board of directors the company ever had consisted of three people—my father, mother and me. Chris Gibson, whom my father hired in 1942 as Raymond's first professional engineer (not to disparage Bill House, the greatest natural engineer I ever knew), was added in the early 1950s as a "promotion without remuneration." That roster remained until 1956, the year we went public, at which time I approached my father. What we now needed, I told him, was an "outside board" made up of business leaders from other companies. His response was, "If you think that's what we need, then do it."

I told him I would. My first choice was Tom Wilson, CEO and president of the Marine Midland Bank of Binghamton. Tom, who was my father's age and one of his best friends, was a mentor to me and one of my personal heroes. Prior to his successful business career, he'd fought in World War I, and after that had been a football star at Princeton. In those simpler, by-gone days, the player elected captain by his teammates was also the coach, and in his senior year Tom was captain and coach. He said he'd be pleased to be on the Raymond board.

Another early member was Lou Durland, the treasurer of Cornell University, who was personally responsible for raising the school's endowment from $18 million to nearly $300 million. As often happens on a board, a member suggests someone who he or she thinks would serve well and would add to the board's collective stature. Lou Durland did this for us by suggesting Bob Bass, who worked for Borg Warner and had just been transferred from Ithaca to the company's head office in Chicago. Lou said, "Bob will be the next president of Borg. Better get him while you can."

Bob Bass was a tremendous asset to our board for many years. Another early member was Phil Gerner, a partner in George D. B. Bondbright, the Rochester brokerage house that had done our first public offering. Basically, that was the make-up of our board for the first decade—until my father, having survived pancreatitis in 1950 and two strokes in the early 1960s, died in January of 1967. As the doctor said, "The old guy just wore out." I carried his ashes back to Greene where we held a memorial service, for which the whole community turned out.

At this juncture, I knew I needed a new chairman and asked Tom Wilson if he would accept the job. His reaction surprised me; he seemed suspicious. "I suppose you want me as a replacement for your father," he said.

"Tom, I want you for you and you alone."

"What do you have in mind for me?"

"Simple," I said. "I want to meet with you before each board meeting, say at breakfast the day before. I'll have the agenda all laid out, and I'll want you to go over every item that I intend to propose. Question the hell out of it. If I can't sell you on it, then I'll take it off the agenda."

He smiled at that, and we shook hands. "It's a deal."

Tom Wilson did a great job as our chairman for several years. At our June, 1972, board meeting, he told us that he was about to leave for an African safari. At 82 he was bursting with anticipation and

excitement. When his doctor heard that Tom was planning so strenu-
ous a trip, he insisted on putting him through a complete physical. In
the process he discovered that Tom had cancer of the pancreas.

Tom canceled his trip and began to decline rapidly. We all knew he
didn't have long to live. Shortly before he died, he invited me to his
home in Binghamton. When I arrived he said he had something he
wanted me to take care of.

Every year for almost a decade, Tom had hosted our August board
meeting at his fishing camp on the Delaware River. It was called a
"camp," but it could easily house fifty people. He insisted we have the
August meeting there one last time, even though he would not be
able to attend. I swallowed hard when he said that, then went ahead
with the plans to set things up.

It was a fine meeting, but the specter of Tom's fate hung heavy over
all of us, and before the meeting was over we decided on a course of
action. At my suggestion, we voted to give a block of Raymond
Corporation stock worth $20,000 to Princeton University, to be used
for football scholarships. Business attended to, I barbecued beef ten-
derloins over an open fire using a recipe that featured my own sauce.
It was a great meal, and we lifted a glass to Tom in gratitude and affection. The next day the meeting broke up and I headed back to Greene.

On my way home I stopped at Tom's house and told him what we
had done. In thanking me, he became very emotional, and I could tell
how much our gesture meant to him. Later I would learn that his
own company, Marine Midland Bank of Binghamton, which he'd
built into a powerhouse singlehandedly, did nothing to honor him
until *after* his death.

After Tom died I was reminded of a series of discussions we'd had
on the board some years earlier about setting a mandatory retirement
age for board members. The suggested age was seventy-two. Believing
that the only real criteria for continued service on our board should

be one's ability to do the job, I had fought that proposal vigorously. At Tom's funeral it came to me in a rush: if I had lost that fight, we would have missed ten years of Tom Wilson's outstanding leadership.

One of the best examples of Tom's influence and vision was his recommendation for membership of Dexter Keezer on the Raymond board. At the McGraw-Hill publishing company, where he was a vice president in the 1960s, Keezer was considered the outstanding industrial economist in the country. His book, *The Public Control of Business,* was both a critical and commercial success. Tom Wilson, who was on the McGraw-Hill board, wanted Keezer for our board, but we learned that he was prohibited from serving on any board that advertised, as we did, in a McGraw-Hill publication.

Tom came up with a way to get Dexter to help us without actually joining our board—that is, to help us without money changing hands. He knew that Keezer loved fly fishing and was always on the lookout for opportunities to wet a line on the Delaware. At Tom's suggestion, we worked out a deal whereby The Raymond Corporation paid one-half of Keezer's travel and lodging expenses, and a bookbinding company in Binghamton paid the other half. After three visits, the bindery backed out of the agreement, and Raymond picked up all of Keezer's expenses—and was only too glad to do it! As a result, we were the beneficiary of Dexter's wisdom and counsel at all board meetings for the next fifteen years. I look at it as one of the best "deals" we ever made.

One of the most dramatic examples of the wisdom of Keezer's advice came in 1971 when President Nixon instituted his wage and price freeze. I was slated to take part in an American Management Association roundtable discussion. These gatherings, for which the AMA was famous, featured literally dozens of CEOs from all types of companies sitting around an immense round table, and offering, in turn, their opinions on whatever topics were current at the time. On this occasion, President Nixon had just announced his wage and price freeze, and it was the hottest of the hot topics.

As it happened, the day before this meeting, Dexter Keezer had given the Raymond board his thoughts on the subject, and I was pleased that they were the same as mine. So when it was my turn to speak up at the AMA meeting, after some sixty or seventy business leaders had said the freeze was the right and only thing to do, I said that the policy was both wrong and wrong-headed, wouldn't work, and was the "most foolish thing Nixon could have done." The roomful of men who had preceded me, all of whom represented companies far bigger than The Raymond Corporation, looked at me as if to say, "And who might *you* be?"

As history tells us, the wage-price freeze was not the most successful of Mr. Nixon's domestic policies. The country chafed under the plan. Dexter Keezer called it "the worst thing that could have happened." Based on my experience as an executive who had to follow the freeze, I had firsthand knowledge that it not only didn't work, it also did a lot of harm. Our people accepted it without too much grumbling, but after a year had passed, three men from the shop came to see me.

"George," their leader said, "you have to do something about this. We just can't take it any longer. It's costing us more to live, and our pay is staying the same."

"I understand perfectly," I said, "only I'm not sure what I can do. It's a presidential order."

"Will you try?"

"Of course. I promise you that."

It so happened President Nixon lifted the wage and price freeze the very next day! The three men who'd come to see me quickly spread the word of their visit and my promise to do something about the situation, and before long half the plant thought George

Raymond Jr. was personally responsible for saving the country! The timing was mere coincidence, but the next time I attended an AMA Roundtable meeting I was viewed—and listened to—with considerably greater respect.

The visit of the three men from the plant had a second important aspect. I was still very much in the midst of my learning phase in regard to organizational development and team management, and was thus always looking for feedback. So I said to them, as they sat side by side in my office that day, "Now that you've spoken, let me ask you a question. How come it took three of you to come in here to see me?"

"We're giving each other support," one of them said.

"Support?"

"We were nervous about coming to see you."

You can literally take the door off its hinges, but that still doesn't make it easy for employees to cross the threshold into the president's office. "From now on," I told the three, and after that the rest of the workforce, "if you want to talk, come to see me. But if you don't want to come to my office, I'll come to see you."

And on many an occasion I did.

A board of directors, well chosen, is a fountain of knowledge; much is to be gained if one is open to learning. One of the most interesting and worthwhile things I picked up was Lou Durland's formula for valuing companies. This was in the 1970s, when we were doing extremely well, and I began getting unsolicited offers to buy Raymond out. I had never thought much about that possibility until then, so during a coffee break at one of our board meetings I asked Lou how to determine the fair asking price of a company.

He had a great deal of money at his disposal as the treasurer of Cornell, and huge experience in bringing money in and spending it wisely. At the time, he had served on approximately forty boards, and every time he went on one he bought enough of that company's stock so that he—meaning Cornell—owned 10 percent of the company. Over the years, quite a few of those companies changed hands, and more often than not it was Lou Durland who set—and got—the selling price.

"I'll give a foolproof formula on how to do it," he said, and I knew he was speaking as one who knows. "If a company has had five years of increasing sales and profits, then take its anticipated sales volume for the coming year, and that's the price."

Not long after we'd had that discussion, I didn't hesitate when a friend of mine, Carl Sirriani, who owned a company that made "animal enclosures"—i.e., stainless steel cages—asked me what price he should ask for his company. He gave me his figures and, in a matter of minutes, I told him.

"I'll never get that much!"

"If you don't, you'll still have the company. So what do you have to lose?"

He agreed, somewhat reluctantly, to ask for that price. His buyer jumped at the offer.

Another friend, Don Ahearn, took my advice and sold his company, Universal Instruments in Binghamton, for much more than he'd thought possible. When he'd first gone public, he had offered me, as a member of his board, stock at a special offering, and I bought $6,000 worth. I should be buying twice that much, Don said; his company was definitely going places. No, I said, six thousand was enough for me. Ten years later, when he sold the company, my $6,000 investment turned out to be worth $150,000—and he couldn't resist reminding me, in a good- natured way, that I could have doubled it.

The Breakers Hotel, Palm Beach, Florida, 1973. We were just beginning a three-day meeting of directors, and Bob Bass and I were walking on the beach the first day after lunch. Suddenly he said, "You're worried about something, George."

"I am."

"Personal or business?"

"Business."

"Employee?"

I nodded.

He said, "It's Stan Bryant."

"How did you know?"

"That's why you've got directors. It's our business to know. What's the problem?"

"Sales managers have to do more than glad-hand," I said. "I mean, he's great at that. But there's more to the job than greeting customers at the door!"

"You're thinking of firing him, aren't you?"

"Yes. I just don't know how to go about it. He's my oldest friend in the company."

Bob suggested we raise the topic at the board meeting. So I brought it up that same day, and the recommendation wasn't surprising: Stan Bryant had to go. My inclination was to let him down easily, to talk over his performance in a gentlemanly way. After all, I'd hired him as my replacement as sales manager when I went into the army. In 1946, when I came back, he left the company to go with our Chicago dealer, probably because he knew sales was my job and, in all likelihood, I'd get it back. Seven years later, by then the president, I rehired Stan—as sales manager, and he had been with the company ever since. He was a "local boy," like me, except he did me one better; he'd been born in Greene, and I was merely a six-month-old "import" from Brooklyn. It all boiled down to this: I had to fire him, but I still wasn't sure how.

Dick Beckhard, who had never been on the board but frequently attended meetings, was with us in Palm Beach that weekend. At the meeting he said, "George, there's only one way to do it."

"Keep talking," I said.

"First thing when you get back to Greene, call Stan in and tell him he's not doing his job and has twenty-four hours to gather up his stuff."

"Just like that?"

"If your mind's made up, there's no point getting into a discussion. Nothing that Stan can say will change your mind. I know it'll be hard because you're good friends, with his wife also, but that's what you've got to do."

And it's what I did. Stan looked at me for a moment, in shock, then said, "Can I say something?"

"No. You're gone."

And with that he stood up and stormed out of my office.

I gave him a generous severance package, and he went to work with one of our dealers in North Carolina. From time to time through the years Stan would come to Greene on business, and we'd see each other professionally. Two men in the lift-truck industry. But then one day he walked into my office and said, "George, I've buried the hatchet."

We shook hands, old friends once again.

"How's Eleanor?" I asked. She had flat-out refused to speak to me since I'd fired Stan, which isn't to say she hadn't cursed me repeatedly, to him and others.

"Give it a little more time," Stan said; and sure enough, he was right.

It's often said of CEOs that they have the board in their pocket, that the directors are nothing more than a rubber stamp. I never felt that way. I always listened to what my board said, and I took what they said seriously. It's why we met six times a year. Each meeting was a virtual seminar in business administration and human dynamics, with everyone present, both teacher and student.

I've always been a trusting person, perhaps too trusting. It hurt me later in my career, when people I had considered close friends, whom I had entrusted with the leadership of the company betrayed me. But with my board, for those twenty years I ran the company, it was a wonderful journey of learning, trust and affection.

Whenever I think of those board members, I think this: they were good men, and true.

8

True Colors

I n 1972, I hired Jim Hardy as vice president of manufacturing. I had let his predecessor Don Coulson go, because he couldn't make the transition to computers as the managerial tool of the future—in inventory control, spare parts and production. In those days we had an IBM mainframe that took up a whole room. Printouts were stacked ceiling high in Don's office and inventory cluttered the parking lot. It was hard to tell, looking at us from the street, whether we were a manufacturing plant or a storage facility for steel castings.

At a board meeting a week after I hired Hardy, he presented a list of things he intended to accomplish in his first thirty days. To me, it sounded like a politician's promise, and several board members thought he was whistling in the wind to make a strong first impression. Bob Bass, the second-in-command at Borg Warner, told me afterwards, "The guy's nuts. He won't get all that done in a year!"

But Hardy proved he was a man of his word. He uncoiled inventory, removed bottlenecks on the floor, got products out as scheduled. What's more, he understood computers and how to use them effectively. Coulson had looked on them as a bad dream. Hardy saw the computer as a great boon to modern-day business, a friend and a facilitator. And he took to the team management and organizational development programs energetically, becoming one of the better in-house Grid trainers.

I was particularly impressed by one of his accomplishments. I had been having problems with Chris Gibson, our long-time chief engineer. Chris was a hell of a designer but a poor manager. So one day I went down to his office and asked him a loaded question.

"Chris," I asked, "what part of your job do you like best?"

"Designing," he said, with no hesitation.

"And how much time do you spend on it?"

"About 10 percent."

"What do you do with the rest of the time?"

"I try to manage this damn place!"

I laughed, then said, "How would you like to turn that around—spend 10 percent of your time managing and the rest designing?"

"I'd love it!"

Then I casually mentioned the rest, which just happened to be the heart of my plan: "I'd like to bring Jim Hardy in to manage the engineering department."

Chris gave his hands a clap and said, "Wonderful."

Just as Jim had done with the inventory problem, he moved into the engineering department and had it shipshape in no time. Next, I sent him over to marketing, and before you could say fork-lift he had things humming over there too. He was really something to watch, and I took great pleasure in his success.

Jim Hardy was my main man, and I rewarded him for his performance by promoting him to executive vice president in 1978. About this time he suggested that we begin grooming my sons as future CEOs of the company. He said he believed that he could do this more easily than I could, and offered to take charge of the training. I was all for bringing Pete and Steve along and gave Jim the go-ahead. He called them in and presented them with the idea. Steve was all for it, but Pete said, "No way." He simply refused to compete with his brother, and because Pete didn't buy the idea, Steve opted out as well. So that was that, for now. I was still hopeful that one of my sons—more likely Steve at this point—would eventually take over the top job in the company.

Three years later, in 1981, I decided that Hardy was ready to run the entire show and that I could kick myself upstairs to the board chairmanship. At that time we didn't have the organizational title CEO—but for all intents and purposes, Jim Hardy was now Raymond's chief executive. Jim Hardy had proven himself a capable and effective executive, loyal to the company and dedicated to its growth and success. He "bled orange."

One afternoon, a couple of years after Jim had taken over—with me continuing as chairman of the board—he came to me and asked what I thought of leveraged buyouts. I said I had nothing against them on the surface; a leveraged buyout implied the assumption of considerable debt, which was something to consider. "Why do you ask?"

"George, I'd like to put together a leveraged buyout of the company."

I was surprised but wasn't opposed to the plan. If Hardy could swing it—if he could borrow all the money to buy back all the outstanding Raymond stock—Raymond would become a closely held family company again. About a month later Jim gave me a progress report; on the strength of it I set up a special meeting in Syracuse so he could present the idea to the executive committee of the board. On the morning that we were all to meet in Syracuse, I went to my office in Greene at 7:30; Jim Hardy and the three company executives who were assisting him in the buyout were waiting for me.

Jim said he had to talk to me, so I invited him into my office. I kept my coat on because I was about to get into my car and start driving. Jim stood there looking at me for a moment, then said, "We can't do it."

"How come?"

"The figures didn't work out."

"Well, too bad," I said. "I'll go to Syracuse and tell them the deal's off."

After his plan fell through, something seemed to change in Jim. I began to sense that he was trying to turn the board against me. When I confronted him about it, he said I was letting my imagination run away with me; but the long and the short of it was we had a falling out, and in the fall of 1986 Jim said he was resigning. I took over the president's office again, and six months later I learned what had really happened. The leveraged buyout part was true. What was kept from me was that Hardy's plan was to make *him* the 51 percent owner of the company, with the other 49 percent being shared equally among his partners. I, and the rest of the Raymond clan, were to be bought out; paid for our shares and stripped of all ownership. But Jim couldn't raise the money without me as part of the package, and the deal fell through at the last minute.

And this was the man I had thought bled orange? Alone in my office, after hearing the news, I could only bow my head in hurt and stunned disbelief.

So I was back at it, searching for a new chief executive. Using a high-powered headhunter, I found Bill Weber.

Having arranged his first interview with me in Nantucket, where I now had a summer home, I knew I was going to like him the moment he stepped off the plane, and I did. But liking Bill Weber wouldn't mean anything unless I came to believe he was the man for the job. We talked all that morning and through the best lunch Sconset could offer—at the Summer House; when he left the island later that day, I not only still liked him personally, I admired his background and respected his views on business and management. It occurred to me, as he turned on the tarmac to wave goodbye, that my search for Raymond's next chief executive might well be over.

It was. Once again I stepped aside as president, but this time with a distinct feeling that my career, as a decision-making executive, was over. Though I would stay on as chairman of the board, for all intents and purposes I was retiring. On that occasion, at a party held at the Binghamton City Club in 1987, I spoke about Raymond's new chief executive to the assembled guests:

> I have come to see Bill Weber as having the experience, training, and managerial know-how to guide the Company to its next financial plateau. He managed, with great success, General Electric's major appliance division, with revenues of $500 million. So he would certainly feel comfortable running a company whose sales were slightly over $100 million.
>
> Conceivably I might have wanted someone with a background in capital goods to manage Raymond when the time came for me to step aside—one can't exactly buy a $60,000 lift truck in the local mall! But it was exactly Bill's "consumer" training and experience at G.E. that appealed to me. I viewed him as an executive very much in step with the times, aware of the changes taking place in business and society, knowledgeable of consumers' needs.
>
> Now there is no doubt Raymond manufactures capital goods, but I could not envision a "capital goods" executive leading Raymond in today's—not to mention tomorrow's!—fast-paced, high-tech world. Bill Weber's background in the consumer-oriented General Electric Corporation was just what we needed at Raymond to carry us onward and upward.
>
> Bill is a line manager's manager. He knows his business. And he's a superb planner. I've never met anyone in my forty-five years in the field who plans so well as Bill Weber. Like all successful individuals, he has strong motivation, high personal goals—to be number one, the top. I will not put words in Bill's mouth and say he's worked all these years toward the goal of one day running a company—but if I *did* say that, I don't believe I'd be wrong.
>
> It is this personal drive in all great leaders that instills motivation and spirit in the companies they head—or universities or causes or nations. None of us needs fear that The Raymond Corporation will slow down,

become lazy or complacent, with Bill Weber in charge. He is a man
who directs his tremendous energies into results. If Raymond *can*
become a 200-million-dollar, then a 300-million-dollar, then a 500-
million-dollar company, William R. Weber is the executive who will
make it happen....

....I pass to you, Bill Weber, the mantle of leadership, woven over a
period of sixty-four years from the threads of hard work, dedication,
and deep caring for people. May you wear it in good health as you steer
Raymond, with your own unique blend of vision, patience and verve,
toward the twenty-first Century."

Like Jim Hardy, who was so effective when first coming on board,
Weber had an excellent start. But the honeymoon ended quickly
when, in office less than three months, he began demeaning my personal secretary, Terry Brandt, claiming she was inefficient, careless, and
lackadaisical. At almost every opportunity, he bad-mouthed her to
people in the plant. I told him his comments were inappropriate; in
short, he was wrong about Terry. She was excellent at her job and an
outstanding woman as well. He should keep his comments to himself.

But Weber kept it up, almost as if he were trying to bring me down
by bringing down my secretary. It was the strangest interpersonal
dynamic I had ever experienced, and I finally wrote him a letter, con-
fronting him with his hurtful and destructive campaign and saying
that I was going to take the matter to the board of directors. His reaction was to say it wasn't true.

In June of 1988, Bill Weber and I were to take part in a regular meeting of the board, but we had a preliminary meeting at breakfast with
Bob Bass and Richard Rose, the new chair of the Human Resources
Committee, to try and straighten out our disagreements. Wanting to
avoid the possibility of hand-to-hand combat before the full board, I
laid out the whole situation, making sure to mention the good things
Weber had done; for example, his creation of a series of manuals
describing the duties and responsibilities of the different departments in

the company. I suggested that Bob and Rich pick an outside consultant to facilitate a meeting between me and Bill. They responded favorably to the idea, but Weber flatly refused to participate. So that afternoon the matter was brought before the full board, without Bill Weber or me attending.

The board met for almost two hours. Then they called us in and announced they had set up a committee and charged it with interviewing all the officers and top executives of the company to find out what they thought of Weber. The two men on the committee, Arthur Richardson and Richard Rose, were given thirty days to report back to the full board, but it didn't take long for word to begin filtering in that half the people Richardson and Rose interviewed were getting their resumes up-to-date, and the other half already had them in their back pocket. They were *all* ready to jump ship.

The preponderance of complaints against Weber dealt with his way of verbally abusing an employee, often in front of his or her peers or subordinates. The effect on morale was devastating. As one long-time employee told me, "Before Weber, if someone fell in a hole, his coworkers would be right there. Under Weber, if that happened, everyone would look the other way, fearful of getting involved. We've stopped caring. There's no energy left."

At the second meeting, Richardson and Rose reported to the board, and in less than an hour the decision was made. After occupying the presidency for barely six months at a salary approximating $300,000, Bill Weber was terminated, and had twenty-four hours to clean out his desk and leave the building. Which he did. Not long afterward he filed a suit against the company for breach of contract. There was no way I would pay him a cent. If anyone broke a contract, it was Weber; but my board thought the wise thing to do would be to pay him off, instead of fighting him in court. I hate to part with money that isn't due someone, but that was what we ended up doing—to the tune of almost a million and a half.

That there had been such a drastic change in the culture of The Raymond Corporation was what pained me most about Weber's tenure as president. Ironically, in my remarks welcoming him into the Raymond family, I had said:

> We can never forget that *first,* Raymond is people. People make the business. And that goes back to the days when Greene was a sleepy southern-tier village, and my father only had a handful of employees on the payroll.
>
> This philosophy—that Raymond *is* people—is what has made my job so stimulating and so rewarding during these years. For all our striving and hard work and dedication, we have always been a team—working and pitching in and having fun together. Business can only be truly successful if the people who work hard to make the business, have a good time doing it. That is Raymond's culture. And it is my fervent belief that we must nourish this culture if we are to continue growing, if we are to flourish in the years that lie ahead.

I had always thought myself a good judge of character, but suddenly I didn't know. Or maybe it wasn't my fault at all, but something else—a poison that crept into certain men's veins when they reached the top, twisting their perspectives, warping their ethics. Whatever it was, my first two choices to lead the company were failures. It's an oft-heard expression that power corrupts. I had never believed it but now I was beginning to, having witnessed a pair of top executives reveal their true colors once power was theirs.

I had no choice but to try again. Somewhere out there was an executive who would lead the company into the 1990s with vision, energy and, yes, integrity.

In considering the position, I chose a man who was both a Raymond dealer and a board member, someone I had known for thirty years as head of the Johnston Equipment Company, our

Canadian dealership. As a board member, Ross Colquhoun was at the meeting in Syracuse that began with the termination of Bill Weber and ended with his election as the new president of Raymond.

On the ride back to Greene, where I was to inform our executives and then the rest of the company that Ross Colquhoun was the new chief executive, he turned to me and said, "After you've told management, I think you should leave the meeting. I also think it would be a good idea if you found an office someplace else, preferably in Binghamton. If you're still on the premises, people won't know if an order or a decision is really mine. You remember how it was those last three months with Weber." Surely I did, as I remembered how difficult it had been for me to exercise full authority so long as my father was around.

What he said made sense, and I told him so. Ross smiled and turned to look out the window at the countryside. I looked out my window as well, grateful that the company was in the hands of a caring, strong, principled leader at last.

9

Crime and Punishment

On June 1, 1977, I went home for lunch, which I rarely did. My doctor had put me on a diet in preparation for a series of x-rays, so around noon I left my office and walked out to my car. I stopped at the foot of our long driveway to speak to my trainer about a new colt, then drove the rest of the way up the drive and parked in the garage. As soon as I stepped from the garage into the house, I had the feeling that something was wrong. In the middle of the hallway were two bags of groceries, on the floor. I thought, What's this? Cynnie would never leave groceries here.

I walked down the hall into the family room, which had huge glass doors all along one side. Something caught my eye, and I moved closer. On the floor in front of the sliding doors was a nail file. I glanced at the nearby coffee table and saw that the rest of her manicure things were lying on it neatly arranged, though this was not their usual place. This was getting stranger by the minute.

I called out her name a couple of times, but remembering how much she disliked anyone yelling inside the house, I stopped. I went into the kitchen and got my special lunch from the refrigerator, which Cynnie had said she would prepare for me, and there it was. Oh well. I had a few bites, trying to figure out where she might be. It was a Wednesday, her golf day; but it had rained and was too wet for golf. I began to get very nervous and searched the house, every closet and space where she could possibly be.

Ah, Doris, I thought, the friend Cynnie golfed with every Wednesday. Doris would know. I picked up the phone in the kitchen, and it was dead! Now I really started to panic. Looking out the window, I thought I could see wires hanging from the utility pole in the distance. I went outside and walked across the big turnaround to where the woods began. The ground looked trampled around the utility pole as if someone had recently been there and cut the telephone wires. Jumping into my car, I drove down the hill to the horse barn, and was relieved to find that its phone was working. With a growing sense of fear, I called the police.

I wanted to shout, "My wife is missing!" But not knowing that for certain, I told the officer about my severed phone line, adding that my wife should have been home, and that I had no idea where she was.

I drove back to the house and waited anxiously, but no one came. I went back down to the horse barn, called the police again, and a short time later a state trooper drove up. He got out as if he had all the time in the world, or better things to do.

"What's going on?" he asked, his tone almost haughty.

This time I said it straight: "My wife is missing."

"How do you know that?"

I started to explain about the groceries and the manicure set, but I knew that wouldn't impress him, so I said, "Look at this." I led him over to the window and indicated the telephone pole where the wires had clearly been cut. That got his attention. He went back to his car and made a radio report. Ten minutes later the place was alive with policemen.

The first thing the cops did was to tell me to contact the children and have them come to the house immediately. I did that, and Pete, Steve and his wife, and our daughter Jean hurried over. They had no information about their mother or her whereabouts, and there was nothing I could tell them, so we all sat there waiting quietly, apprehensively.

Sometime that afternoon, a plainclothes county policeman came in, took me aside, and asked me to sit down. For almost an hour, he quizzed me as to anything and everything I could remember that might be helpful. Assuming this was all routine, I thought nothing of his questions and answered them as directly and as best I could. Then he got up, abruptly, and just walked away. After that, the kids and I were basically quarantined. We were told we could leave the house, but only to walk on the deck for fresh air if we felt the need. We were not to leave the premises.

I noticed there was a cop stationed at the bottom of the hill, and I could see other officers here and there. But it was not until much later that I learned they had a force of policemen in and around the village, as many as 130 for more than a week. My downstairs office became their on-site command post, with another one in the village as the main command post.

After dinner that evening I dozed off in a chair in the family room. Suddenly there was a loud knock on the glass door. I went over to it and found two men, a very tall one and the other quite short, both dressed casually in jeans and sport shirts.

I didn't know what they wanted, so was unsure of whether or not to let them in. Two policemen were downstairs in my office. Should I call them first?

At that point, both men flashed wallets and something shiny passed before my eyes. "We're FBI," they said. "Let us in."

I did, and wondered afterwards why I did so without any hesitation or question. By the time they were inside, I'd recovered my composure a bit, and asked to see their IDs again. They complied, and I satisfied myself they were who they said they were.

"Where's your car?" one of them asked, skipping all chitchat.

I led them to the garage and showed them which one was mine. The agent who'd spoken first said, "You can leave us now. We'll be working all night tearing your car apart. But don't worry, we won't hurt anything, and when we give it back to you tomorrow you won't notice anything different."

I asked why they were going to do this and was told, "This appears to be a kidnapping, which is why we were called in. We expect you'll get a ransom note, and when you do, we want to be able to trace your movements. The gadgets we'll put in your car tonight will enable us to do that electronically. It'll make things easier for us—and safer for you."

I left them to their work and went back to the family room to find the chief of police waiting for me.

"George, how much cash money can you lay your hands on?"

"I don't know. Why?"

"Because if you get a ransom note you've got to have the money ready."

"How much are you talking about?" I asked.

"I'd suggest a million dollars."

"When should I get it?" was my only question.

"As fast as you can."

"And then bring it back here?"

"Yes. We want it available."

I called my friend Hart Morse, the president of the Marine Midland Bank in Binghamton, and made the arrangements. Two hours later, six men from the bank showed up at my door, each with a briefcase strapped to his right wrist. They waited, nervously but politely, while I counted the money—most of it in small denominations. The counting took some time, but I finally finished and the men from the bank left, taking their briefcases with them. I put the money, all one million dollars of it, in a big cardboard box I had in the office, and shoved it out of sight in the furnace room, right next door to where the cops were sitting. Surely it would be safe there.

The next morning, the chief asked me how many volunteers I could get to help search the hundreds of acres of woods surrounding the house.

"How many do you want?"

"Five hundred would do it."

"I can get that many right down at the plant." I called Jim Hardy, my vice president of manufacturing, who was running the operation in my absence, and asked him if he could get that many people to volunteer a couple hours of their time.

"Sure," he said, and a half hour later he called back to say he had them all lined up and ready to go.

Out they came, in a convoy of buses, and were immediately deployed by the police, shoulder to shoulder in a single line, all across the woods. They used light string to keep everyone in line and not wandering off, and step by step they walked the entire two miles of woods. They found any number of odd things, including a set of WWII dog tags.

They also found one clue. A piece of masking tape with lipstick on it.

When one of the cops asked me if my wife had more than one shade of lipstick I thought he was kidding. Then I realized he wasn't; he just wasn't married. Cynnie had quite a collection, but there was no need to examine every shade. The lipstick we found on her dressing table, standing apart from the other tubes, appeared to be a match.

Shortly after that I heard a huge whirring sound like something out of a war movie. I ran to the window and saw a police helicopter landing in an open space next to the house. That was how they had arranged to send the tape and the tube of lipstick to the police lab in Albany, the state capitol, for tests. The next day the lab verified that the lipstick stain on the tape had come from the tube on her dressing table. According to the police, there was now no doubt that it was a kidnapping. Then why weren't we hearing from the kidnapper?

The children and I settled in to wait, hoping the police would soon find Cynnie, safe and unharmed. We wanted news instantly—as long as it was good news. But, in truth, we didn't know what to think, whether a long wait was good or bad. Every time the phone rang we jumped.

Then the phone stopped ringing, or at least the people calling didn't have the news we so desperately wanted to hear.

Several days passed. We were sitting in the family room, bored and very unhappy, when a state trooper drove up to the house and brought me a drawing done by a state police artist.

It was a composite drawing of a car, a bluish-gray sedan, based on information the agency had received. I was asked if I knew that car or had ever seen it before, and I had to answer no to both questions. It turned out that among 3,000 interviews the police had conducted, they had talked to a farm couple who had seen a car like this parked on a dirt road near their property. And they'd seen it not just once, but twice! Yet when the police interviewed the couple, neither husband nor wife mentioned the car, not wanting to "get involved"; they only came forward when some friends urged them to. When they did so, several days later, they told the police that the car was there one day, gone the next, and then back again briefly on the third. What made this information valuable was that the woods leading up to our house began directly where they had seen the car.

At first I got excited, but when days went by and nothing happened, I thought we'd reached yet another dead end. But the police persisted, expanding their search for the owner of the car in ever-widening circles until, on the fifth day after my wife's disappearance, they learned the owner's name, and that he was a twenty-seven-year-old Vietnam vet living in Whitney Point, a small town 11 miles away. He had a troubled employment history and a failed marriage. In addition, the police learned that the man had gone to his daughter's school and taken her out of class, apparently on his way out of town, in an old bluish-gray Ford.

I was sitting in my downstairs office at home when a ranking officer of the state police walked in and said he had something to tell me. I knew it was serious by his tone and expression. He paused a lengthy moment, and my heart stood still. God help me, I thought. Quietly the gray-uniformed trooper spoke. It wasn't a kidnapping. A search party had found my wife in the woods; she was dead.

I hunched over in my chair, let out a gut-wrenching groan, and began to cry uncontrollably. For how long I don't know, but finally I collected myself, looked up, and the officer filled me in with more information.

They had located the man in Tennessee the day after he'd left town. While the police were interrogating him, they were also searching his car. What they didn't tell the man, at first, was that they had found Cynnie's body on the same day they had picked him up in Tennessee. When confronted with details of the crime, he had broken down and confessed. The man was now in New York State, in the county jail awaiting a court appearance. One of my board members, William Lyon, president of New York State Electric & Gas, had sent his company plane to Tennessee to bring him back.

Shocked as I was, devastated as I felt, I knew it was an amazing piece of police work and thanked the officer for being so forthright with me. He thanked me, in turn, for my cooperation, offered his condolences, then said I could inform my children of their mother's death. Which I did, one at a time. Quite simply, it was the hardest thing I'd ever done in my life.

Not long afterward, while officers were still in my house, the same trooper who had broken the news to me of Cynnie's murder, said, "George, did you ever wonder why we spent so much time interviewing you, why we asked you so many questions?"

"You were probably hoping I'd think of something significant I might have forgotten."

"Well," he said, "that was part of it, but the main reason we questioned you was because you were a prime suspect."

"I was?"

"In cases like this, the surviving spouse is always questioned extensively."

"Were you thinking of arresting me?" I asked.

"Not after the first two days." He smiled. "We decided you were in the clear."

"Well, thanks for telling me," I said, smiling myself—for the first time in a week.

We held Cynnie's funeral in the Episcopal Church in Greene, and all the people who'd wanted to come by during the horrible week from June 1st to June 7th—between the disappearance and the discovery—but had been turned away at the bottom of the drive, showed up in force. I "decreed" that the internment would be private, just for the family, but after that everyone would be welcome back at the big house on the hill.

People came from Binghamton, Norwich, New York City, Philadelphia, Alfred, Ithaca—everywhere, it seemed. All day long they streamed in and out of the house, until finally at six o'clock the traffic slowed, then stopped altogether. I looked around and it was just me and the kids—and the cop left on duty "just in case," the policeman I had come to like and respect so much. Before the evening was over, I told him that he had a real talent for kindness, for helping people get through a trying time, and that my children and

I were very grateful to him personally.

His response surprised me. He said, quietly but with great emotion, "This is the last time I'll do this kind of thing, George. I've come to feel like a member of the family, and I never want to go through it again."

That same night, I did something that, in retrospect, perhaps I shouldn't have done. I looked at my three children and said, "I'm scared, kids. Damn scared. I'm not a loner. The thought of spending the rest of my life alone terrifies me."

By the expression on their faces, especially Jean's, I knew what they were thinking. Do you mean you're going to start looking for someone to take Mom's place?

I didn't answer. Nothing more on the topic was said. But the answer was yes.

That same evening Dick Beckhard showed up and took charge. First, he sat down with the family and said wise and kindly things to all of us. For the first time in my long observation of Dick and his methods, he gave direct specific advice to each one of us, all of which added up to: "Honor Cynnie's memory, but get on with your lives, and as quickly as possible."

He gave each one of the children a specific, time-consuming task to do. He told Pete to get rid of Cynnie's car—"I don't care what you do with it, sell it or give it away, but get it out of the garage and out of the county, so your father won't have to see it ever again." Jean was to get rid of all of her mother's personal things in the house and bathrooms, especially the night clothes, and Steve and his wife were to distribute, or dispose of, the rest of her belongings. As for me, he said I should attend an annual conference he held at MIT in Boston, then two weeks away. There would be ten or twelve couples there for lectures in a very relaxed setting. "I think you'd better plan to be there, George," Dick went on. "You don't have to come to any of the sessions if you don't feel like it—just sit around the pool all day if that's what you want. But it would do you good to be near other people. And away from here."

The next day Dick and I drove to the plant. He told staff and workers alike what to expect when I came back—that I would probably break down on occasion and perhaps cry, and there was absolutely nothing wrong with this; it was a perfectly normal and healthy response to what I'd gone through. When the time came to go back to my office—three days later—I did, in fact, cry, and they handled it beautifully.

Before Cynnie's death if anyone had asked me what kind of father I'd been, I would have said a good one. I tried to emulate, with my children, the relationship I'd had with my own father. I thought he would be a good model, a fine standard to shoot for. I did the best I could and, frankly, I thought I'd done pretty well. But the violent death of their mother, at age fifty-five, had a devastating effect on our kids. Looking back, I would say that the boys recovered fairly well and, all things considered, relatively quickly, but it took Jean ten long, hard years, and even to this day I think she bears the scars of that horrid day in June.

From the earliest days of our marriage Cynnie and I had a cottage on a nearby lake, and the kids just loved it. I had bought an old boat with an outboard motor that I reworked for Pete, my oldest, which in time got handed down to Steve and finally to Jean. We encouraged them to bring their friends, and there were always scores of kids running around, in and out of the water. It was close to idyllic.

While the children were young and Cynnie was busy raising them, she belonged to the PTA. Later, when they were older, she was active with the town library. Greene had a wonderful library and a librarian who was simply terrific, but the dear woman was underpaid and overworked and often on the verge of quitting. So Cynnie and a friend stepped in and volunteered to help. It saved the day, and the library. Remembering this, one of the things I did following her death was to let her friends know that instead of sending flowers, the family would appreciate their making donations to a fund in her memory. They did, and their contributions totaled almost $18,000, which I matched for a grand sum of more than $35,000 dollars.

We used the money to refurbish two rooms in the town library's basement, one for ballet practice and the other as a reading room. These rooms, which are still operating today, are called the Cynthia Raymond Rooms. Actually, there are three Cynthia Raymond Rooms—two in the Greene library, and the third 120 miles away at Alfred University, established with money I donated to the school, where I was a board member for twenty years and chairman for five.

Acting on Dick Beckhard's suggestion, I went to the conference at Endicott House in Boston in late June. It was a combination of information and relaxation, and I took advantage of both to the fullest.

I thought and I thought, lay in the sun for a while and then thought some more. And when I was done, I had a list of twelve items that were central to my future life and happiness. At the top was "finding someone with whom I can share the rest of my life." It was similar to what I had told my children; and here it was again. I didn't want to spend the next year, as society expected, in quiet isolation. Was that view disrespectful of the woman I had loved for so long? I hoped not, and I believed not. I think Cynnie would have said, "George, I know you miss me and love me, but life goes on. Start living it."

Like so many other couples in small towns all across America, my wife and I had a regular routine for our social life. Every week, on either Friday or Saturday night, we would get together with the same five couples, all of whom had done well in one field or another and lived in or near Greene. A number of the men, myself included, went horseback riding on Sunday mornings.

It was a pleasant and congenial group, but it was never the same, at least not for me, after Cynnie was gone. As soon as there were no longer two of us, I lost my "membership" in the group. I'd heard that sort of thing happens following a divorce, that people choose one "side" over the other, but this particular break was as unwanted as it was unplanned.

The annual meeting of the material-handling industry was held in early December that year in San Juan, Puerto Rico. I decided to go. I was a past president twice over, and Cynnie and I had always gone and always had a good time, especially on the first night, which was a black tie dinner for past presidents and their wives. It would actually be a way of honoring her memory, attending the first annual meeting since her death. I had sent notices of her passing to every member in the organization, and had received many heartfelt expressions of sympathy.

In years past, on the first night of the meeting, we'd always sat with George and Pat Millington, a wonderful couple from Philadelphia. When I got to the event this time, I looked around the reception, hoping to spot George and his gracious wife. I was conscious of the looks, and sounds, of surprise caused by my presence; apparently, no one had thought I would come. I didn't see the Millingtons, but when I entered the dining room, they were the first people to greet me.

"Oh, George, I'm so sorry," Pat said, giving me a warm embrace.

"Thank you."

"Who are you having dinner with?" George asked.

"You, I hope."

The Millingtons said they wanted to hear the whole story of Cynnie's death. So I told them what had happened.

When I finished, there was a long silence. Then, to lighten the mood, Pat asked if I had any specific plans for the future. I told her I would very much like to find a nice woman with whom I could spend the rest of my life.

Pat's face lit up. "I'm so happy to hear that, George. I really thought you'd become a confirmed bachelor!"

"Heavens, no," I said.

"Look," she was warming to a task she obviously liked, "if you're going to get married, you have to meet people—that means socializing, going places."

"That's true."

"I don't think there are too many single women in Greene you'd be interested in marrying. Are there?"

"No."

"So come to Philadelphia as our house guest. We're giving back-to-back Christmas cocktail parties later this month, on the 17th and 18th of December. I'll invite every widow and divorcee and unattached gal on the north side of Philadelphia!"

"Sounds great. I'll be there," I said.

And I went. Amazingly enough, I met a wonderful woman that weekend, a beautiful, vivacious brunette from Chicago. Driving back to Greene Monday morning, I was full of excitement and joy. A couple of days later, three of my Greene friends and I made our annual Christmas-buying trip to Drazen's department store in Binghamton. I first stopped at Van Cott's Jewelry Store and bought myself a Rolex Oyster wristwatch and later, at Drazen's, a black, silver-trimmed, ankle-length velour bathrobe. While my friends were buying gifts for their wives, I got on the phone to Chicago; and a very nice conversation it was.

At a New Year's Eve party—my first New Year's since Cynnie's death—an overt break occurred between me and my old Greene friends. Determined not to stay at home, I took my daughter, Jean, and we both enjoyed ourselves. I showed a few friends a photograph of the woman I'd met in Philadelphia, who had been in my thoughts ever since, though I didn't say that to anyone—especially my kids. But it was true, and I was very proud of the picture, which she had sent me.

As I was getting a fresh drink at the New Year's party, one of my pals from the old weekend group, Carl Siriani, came up to me and said, "Your friends have been talking to me, George. They don't think it's wise for you to be showing pictures of a 'new woman' at this time. The trial is next month, and people have a way of putting two and two together. If you know what I mean."

Perhaps my exuberance had carried me away. I was willing to grant him that. But I didn't like his judgmental tone, and I decided right then that I really didn't like him very much either. "Don't tell me what people think!" I said back to him, sharply. "It's *you* who's thinking it, and don't tell me what to do—or what not to do!" With that, I turned my back on him and walked away.

The next day was New Year's Day. For years Cynnie and I had hosted a huge party, starting with the Rose Bowl Parade and ending with the game itself. My "pal" of the night before showed up with his wife, and when he saw me he gave me a sheepish look, as if to say, "Is it all right for us to be here?" I nodded at him and said hello to her, but avoided them for the rest of the afternoon. I had already gotten the impression that my three kids, when you got right down to it, thought I should be a grieving widower for the rest of my life. In a way, I'd expected that from them—but not from my friends in Greene. My life was changing. I could feel myself breaking away from old patterns, seeking new horizons.

At long last the trial began on February 2, 1978. As came out in testimony, the defendant had attended Greene High School, where he'd been in the same class as Steve, our younger son. After selecting

Cynnie as his victim, he had watched her until he had a good idea of her routines, then surprised her on the morning of June 1st. He taped her mouth shut, push-walked her through the woods to the spot on the road where he'd left his car, then put her in the trunk and drove to an abandoned farm. Once there, he took her out of the trunk, walked her into a wooded area, made her kneel on a prayer rug he'd brought back from Vietnam, and shot her with a sawed-off shotgun. Then he just left her there in the open.

What was his motive? This insane man had a "plan," an insane plan. He had interviewed for the job of chief of police of nearby Whitney Point but failed to get it, so he came up with a scheme. He would murder a prominent person, then leave town. When the crime remained unsolved, he would come back to town, solve it, and be made chief of police. Would he solve it by framing some innocent person? Did he think he could solve it by incriminating himself and then serving as police chief from prison? It never made any more sense than his senseless act which took my beloved wife and the children's mother from us.

At the trial he denied all of this, saying the police had the wrong man. But he had confessed soon after his arrest in Tennessee, and now the judge ruled that his confession was admissible. Certain friends and family members, my daughter Jean, for one, attended the entire trial. As for me, I testified as required, then went back to work—except for the last day when I returned to hear the verdict. The man was found guilty of kidnapping in the first degree and murder in the second degree.

Cynnie's killer was led away, hands cuffed behind his back, head bowed. I didn't feel one ripple of joy or satisfaction, just a very deep sadness. I could only wonder at the pointlessness of the whole gruesome business, the sheer insanity of it, and the grief and trauma it had caused me and my children. He wanted to be a police chief so he killed Cynnie? It didn't make sense and I knew it never would. At sentencing, the man received consecutive twenty-year terms for each charge, with parole possible after completion of the first twenty years. At this writing—twenty-two years later—he is in Elmira State Prison serving the second twenty-year term.

As I walked out of the courtroom with my daughter that cold February day, I fought back tears of great pain and loss, even as I looked forward to a new beginning in my life. Much had changed, much had passed; much, thank God, lay ahead.

10

New Horizons

I n the weeks before the Millingtons' back-to-back Christmas parties, I got a number of calls from Pat. At first, she was simply making sure I was serious about coming, but then she started telling me about this "special person" from Chicago who she hoped would be flying out for the weekend.

Her name was Robin Ylvisaker. At first she had told Pat it was too far to travel, especially in this terrible winter weather, then had said maybe, and at last had given Pat a firm yes. Pat was delighted by the prospect that Robin and I would be meeting, but since I'd never even seen a picture of Robin Ylvisaker, my enthusiasm hardly matched hers. To me, she was an unknown quantity. I was excited about meeting all of the single women who would be at the Millingtons' party.

Three days before I left for Philadelphia, I got one last phone call from Pat. She asked when I was planning to get to their house on Saturday, and I said, "About four."

"Could you make it earlier?" she asked.

"How much earlier?"

"Two o'clock."

I told her I could, and I walked through the door at exactly 2:00. George Millington met me at the door and took my suitcase, then led me into their living room where two loveseats faced a stone hearth that held a blazing fire. It had been a tough drive, through rain mixed with snow, and the only thing more inviting than the fire was the beautiful woman sitting next to Pat in one of the loveseats.

"Robin," my host said, "this is George Raymond."

"I'm very happy to meet the 'special person' from Chicago," I said.

Robin gave me a lovely smile, and right away I felt a connection, a certain chemistry, between us. I sat opposite her and the four of us talked openly and easily for the next twenty minutes. I began to see that Robin was indeed special. For one, her looks captivated me—her rich, coal-dark hair, high cheekbones, the fullness of her lips and those warm brown eyes. I could hardly keep my eyes off her. But what I found equally exciting was her personality. This woman was alive, physically and mentally exciting; she radiated energy as she spoke of her childhood in Woodstock, New York, her college years at Smith, the four children she had with her first husband, three girls and a boy. Just then the help who'd been hired for the party arrived. Pat and George excused themselves, and Robin and I were alone.

She gave me a quiet, compassionate look. "Pat told me a little of what happened to your wife."

I nodded. Robin asked me if I cared to talk about it and I told her I didn't mind. The truth was, I already felt comfortable with her, as if I'd known her for years. She patted the cushion beside her and I crossed the small space between us, sat down next to her and began to talk, telling her the story from start to finish, not without a few tears. By all appearances, she was deeply moved and saddened—and in no small way horrified. I told her she was a great listener and she said, "You gave me a whole lot to listen to. My goodness, George, what an awful thing!"

"The trial starts in February," I said.

"God bless you and your children."

"Thank you, Robin."

Her story couldn't compare to mine, she said, although her divorce was painful for her and her children. After many years of trying hard to make her marriage work, she finally had to face up to the inevitability of its end. She and Bill had had their time, but in recent years communications had broken down between them and he had run off with a woman their daughter's age! When she said that, sparks of anger flashed in her eyes. I told her that I believed, in a certain sense, divorce was actually harder to live with than death, and she was interested to learn why I felt that way. My loss was final, I said. Cynnie was taken by some bizarre twist of fate. Dwelling on what had already happened was pointless, perhaps psychically unhealthy. But because of Robin's children, she would always have to have dealings with Bill, their father, and would be continually reminded of the anger and hurt the breakup had caused her.

"There's something to that," she said pensively. "Still, I wouldn't wish what you went through on anyone!"

Outside it had started snowing and I felt relaxed and happy sitting with Robin. If she felt happy and relaxed sitting with me, I didn't know, but she wasn't jumping up and running away! "You must have loved your wife a great deal," she said.

"I did, very much."

She smiled wistfully. "I just can't imagine Bill ever shedding a tear over me!"

I didn't say anything. I was thinking the man must have a real problem, leaving so lovely a woman as this. I saw Pat coming back into the room. Before she got to us, I said, "You know, Robin, I have never talked with anyone like this before."

"Hey you two, it's five o'clock. The party starts at 5:30 and you aren't dressed yet. Get going."

We both ran up the stairs. The room Robin was staying in was at the head of the stairs and mine was down the hall. I wondered, as I

shed my clothes and headed for the shower, how Robin would compare with Cynnie when it came to getting ready.

I could never fault my wife for not being on time; she always was.
But in order to do so she would have to start a good hour and a half
before we had to leave. I was still thinking about that as I left the room
and, buttoning my sports coat, hurried down the hallway toward the
stairs. To my great surprise, there was Robin, ahead of me, looking
gorgeous in a sequin shirt and black silk pants.

From time to time, as the party progressed, I noticed Robin out
of the corner of my eye. Then, at one point, as she hurried past me
to take a telephone call, she touched my arm lightly and asked,
almost provocatively, "How long do you think it takes to get to know
someone?"

And I answered without skipping a beat, "The rest of your life."

With that, she continued on. We didn't have a chance for anything
more than a word or two after that because of all the other people. It
was, as Pat Millington had predicted, a great party. I talked with a
number of interesting men and women. Then, at about eight, the flow
began to ebb, and soon there were only six of us—Pat and George,
Robin and I, and one other couple. We had a light supper, and then
the other couple left. The four of us chatted for a while in front of the
fire, and then the Millingtons excused themselves, saying they had to
host a repeat of the same party tomorrow night!

Robin and I kept right on talking. Her father had been the
novelist, Henry Morton Robinson, author of *The Cardinal,* and she
described what growing up with him was like. In part exciting,
fun-filled. Every summer, they would put on plays, frequently those
her father had written. Her "greatest role" at the age of fifteen was Jo
in *Little Women.* But growing up with her father was not all fun. In
many ways he was a taskmaster. On one occasion when she was
about ten he returned a letter to her that she had sent him when he

was in the hospital; it was a childish letter, Robin told me, merely saying she hoped he was fine, and he had written in the margin, "I expect more from you. This is very ordinary." I thought it was a cruel thing for her father to do and I told her so. She didn't disagree but she also said it taught her a lesson she never forgot. For the rest of her life she would never again take language, especially the written word, lightly. I liked the positive spin she put on her life experiences, much as I did on mine. I also realized that we'd both had autocrats for fathers.

About midnight, I asked her what she would like for breakfast.

She gave me a look I couldn't quite decipher. Was there something improper in my question? Then she said, "Oh, coffee and juice."

The next morning I got up, dressed and went downstairs. I put coffee and toast and a glass of juice on a tray and walked up and knocked on Robin's door. She was sound asleep, but she woke up and told me to come in. I went in with the tray. She looked at it—and me—as if she didn't believe what she was seeing.

We talked for another hour and a half. She wanted to know what kind of boyhood I'd had. I told her I'd gone to Greene High School, played varsity football and had also acted, starring in a play called *The Valiant*. At that, her eyes lighted up! What else? she wanted to know. So I rambled on, telling her I'd worked in my father's company as a fourteen-year-old, drawing pictures of parts, like hex nuts, in the old drafting room—I'd taken mechanical drawing in high school. Outside of school and work, I fished in the summer, hunted in the fall and trapped muskrats in the winter in Geneganslet Creek. Robin said I sounded like an "All-American boy," and I had to laugh. Then we heard movement in the house, so she sent me downstairs, but not before asking me if I would like to take a walk with her. I told her I loved walking. "Then let's take a great walk somewhere," Robin said. "I'll be right down."

It was only on the streets of Philadelphia but I enjoyed every step of it. She talked about her German-born mother, who still lived in Woodstock and made beautiful braided rugs, and about her sister and brother, both younger. Robin asked me what else I did beside run a company. I said I didn't "run" Alfred University in Alfred, New York, but I was chairman of the board of trustees and helped formulate policy. At the moment I was in the middle of a big fund-raising drive; getting alumni to give money to Alfred was high on my current agenda. I really enjoyed the work I did for the university and liked the association with higher education, especially at a university that had a fine business school.

That night it was the same thing all over again. New faces, new women to meet. But I only had eyes for Robin. Once again, we stayed up after everybody else had gone. It was wonderful, and I knew, before we said good night, that I wanted to see her again. I didn't want it to end here in the Millingtons' beautiful house. For the first time since Cynnie's death I was feeling alive and having fun.

Robin had to go back to Chicago the next morning. I asked her, as we said good night, when she was leaving.

"At six."

"I'll get up."

"Oh, don't. It's much too early."

"But I'd like to say goodbye."

"I'll come in and say goodbye to you."

I woke up early, at 5:15, wondering if she would knock on my door. Perhaps she had just said she would so she could get away without any awkwardness. I thought of the old expression, "Don't call me, I'll call you." It wasn't a very comfortable thirty minutes for me, and when my watch read 5:50 I decided to get up and find out for myself. That same moment there came a light knock on my door. It was the sweetest sound I'd ever heard. I don't know if I fooled Robin into thinking I was asleep, but I rubbed my eyes and stifled a yawn when she came in. It was a short, but marvelously sweet, goodbye.

After she left for the airport, with our host, George, as it happened, I packed my bag for the drive home, then went downstairs to have breakfast with Pat. The first thing I said when I saw her in the kitchen was, "Pat, you've really done it."

"Say that again."

"That's the woman for me."

"I was hoping for something good to come out of this weekend, but, frankly, I'm bowled over."

"So am I," I said, pouring myself a cup of coffee.

She laughed. "Well, good luck. She's one popular lady. Now, how about some scrambled eggs and sausages?"

The drive to Greene, that same day, was a breeze. I thought about Robin the whole way and couldn't wait to call when I got home. I arrived shortly before 3:00, and did just that; she was out, but just hearing her voice on the answering machine was a thrill.

In the next week I must have called Robin four times a day, and on one of our conversations she told me that she was going to Baja for two weeks over Christmas with her friend, a man named Bill, a lawyer in Chicago. I did my best not to dwell on that bit of news but I couldn't totally ignore it, couldn't wipe it completely from my consciousness. It was like a pebble in your shoe, not big enough to make you sit down, untie your shoe and take it out; but you still knew it was there and it wasn't any fun.

In any case, I was scheduled to go on a skiing trip to Canada with my daughter, Jean. Initially, my sons, Pete and Steve, were supposed to come along—I'd rented an apartment in a chalet in Montre St. Anne from a business friend. I thought it would be great for all of us to get away, beneficial to us individually and as a family. But the night before we were to leave, Pete called to say he wouldn't be making it, and an hour later I got the same call from Steve. Both were just too busy. So Jean and I went alone.

We made the drive in my two-seater Ford pickup, and it was one long drive. At first I thought that was why she was so quiet, but soon it became obvious that it was not the duration of the trip but her mood, her frame of mind generally. The trip took much longer than I had expected. The last two hours were interminable. When we got there, things took a turn for the worse. My business friend had somehow double-booked the chalet, and the other family was already there. So Jean and I had to move in with my friend and his family, and his kids had to sleep on the floor to free up beds.

The next day we hit the slopes and it was great skiing, but Jean continued to sulk. By the end of the week, her mood had gone from bad to worse. Finally we had it out. I had been writing letters to Robin all week long, sometimes two a day, and Jean resented the time I would spend with pen in hand writing to a woman so soon after her mother's death. Adding to the problem was that I had recently told her that the living arrangement at home that we had agreed upon was coming to an end. Shortly after Cynnie's funeral, she had said she wanted to quit her job, give up her apartment, and move in with me in the family house. I had agreed, but said it should only be for six months, till January. Then she would be on her own again.

All of this was weighing heavily on Jean over the Christmas holidays. Of the three children, she, the youngest at twenty-five, was the one having the hardest time coming to grips with her mother's death. And with the fact that I wasn't going to spend the next year or two in mourning. I'd made that very clear to them shortly after the funeral, when I'd told them that I didn't intend on being alone for the rest of my life, by myself. Perhaps I was being unduly self-centered, and I now know that one of the truly tragic facets of a real tragedy is the isolation it brings to every individual it touches—the feeling that no one could possibly be as hurt as oneself, nor need and deserve someone else's love in order to recover.

As soon as I got back from Canada I called Robin, who'd just returned from Baja. "This is George," I said.

"George?"

All I could think was, How soon they forget! "George Raymond."

"I know, I'm just kidding," she said with a laugh. "What a nice surprise."

That made me feel a little better. "How was your trip?" I asked, hoping she'd answer, "Awful, terrible—I missed you!"

"Just fabulous. We had this charming villa overlooking the sea."

"Terrific. Listen, will you have dinner with me tonight?"

"Where are you?"

"Chicago."

"Chicago!"

"Well, not yet anyway. But I'll catch the next plane out of Binghamton and can be there by six. How about it?"

When she said, "Great," my heart did a somersault. I told her I'd be staying at the Hotel Tremont and asked her if she could meet me there.

No one had ever seen me leave my office at The Raymond Corporation so fast. At home, I packed a bag and made a beeline for the airport.

When Robin knocked on my door at the Tremont, I took the liberty of giving her a welcoming hug—a kiss didn't seem quite appropriate. That didn't mean I didn't want to! I told her it was wonderful seeing her again. We went down to the bar for a drink, and were barely settled in our chairs when Robin said she had something she wanted to talk to me about.

"Fire away," I said, half-knowing what was coming. I took a quick second sip of my drink.

"George, I'm very glad you're here," she said, then paused. "But I want you to know I'm not exactly 'free.' I've been in a long-term relationship with someone, and I just want you to know about it."

"Don't worry about it," I said with a smile. "Here's the way I look at it. I know it's true in business, and it has to be true in personal relationships. Nothing ventured, nothing gained. Pat told me you were a very popular woman, and look, Robin, here I am anyway." Then I asked her where she'd like to have dinner.

Her response surprised me. "My kids are home for Christmas, and we have a beef stew simmering. Why don't you come see where I live and meet my family?"

I accepted gladly. About an hour later—including the time it took to stop so I could pick up a bottle of wine—we entered her apartment on Lakeview Avenue, overlooking Lincoln Park. While Robin was checking on the stew, I was in the living room with her oldest daughter, Laurie, who immediately got down to issues. Like mother, like daughter, I thought.

"George," she said, "rumor has it you're quite fond of my mother."

"Rumor?"

"OK, then," she said. "The number of times you call her, morning, noon and night."

I laughed. "In this instance the 'rumor' is 100 percent correct. Is that all right with you?"

She told me, with a smile in her cool blue eyes, that it was fine with her. I kind of felt I had passed a test, crossed a first hurdle successfully.

In addition to Laurie, I also met two of her three other children, son Billy and young daughter Amy, at ten the only one still at home (the middle daughter, Beth, was in England at the time). Amy had retreated to her room upon my arrival, but finally gave in to her curiosity and came out to say hello. What a bundle of red-haired joy! Billy had a wonderful, mature bearing. He loved polo, and played at the University of Virginia; as a horseman myself we had a lot to talk about. All in all it was a great evening, and Robin's beef stew—her mother's recipe, she told me—was better than any meal we could have had in any of Chicago's finest restaurants.

Later that evening I kissed Robin at her door. "I've never had a sweeter evening," I said.

I visited Robin every weekend for the rest of the month. Whether I was making any headway with her, I couldn't say. She wasn't telling me she was in love with me, but then she wasn't telling me to stay home. I had the feeling something was changing in her relationship with the lawyer, Bill. Was it cooling down, dying out? Did I have anything to do with it? All I knew for certain was that Robin welcomed me affectionately every Friday when I knocked on her apartment door, and we kept having better and better times together. I took as a particularly favorable sign that she suggested, on my fourth visit, that I bunk in her guestroom; to keep staying at the Tremont was just plain silly, and expensive. I particularly liked waking up in the morning and bringing her breakfast in bed, as I'd done at the Millingtons'. There was no doubt in my mind that we were getting closer and closer. During the week I would call her three times a day, sometimes just to chat with her, sometimes to make plans for the weekend.

On my fifth visit to Chicago, as Robin and I were sitting in her living room having a cocktail, I set down my drink, crossed her lemon-yellow carpet, knelt down in front of her, and asked her to marry me.

"My goodness, George!" She laughed, more nervously, it occurred to me, than joyously. "You don't even know me!"

"Oh, but I do," I told her. "I love you, Robin. Will you?"

She asked me, still smiling, to get off my knees. We should finish our drinks, she said, then talk about it over a nice dinner out. That was fine by me. It had taken a certain amount of courage to "pop the question," and even though she hadn't jumped to say yes, she knew my intentions. I wanted to make Robin my wife.

At dinner she said, "I'm not ready, George. It's as simple as that."

"Is it because of Bill?"

"No. That I can tell you with complete honesty."

"Maybe one day you'll be ready," I said.

She said she hoped that would be so, a warm smile in her eyes, and we didn't mention it again that evening.

An interesting thing happened the next day. Robin decided to have seven or eight couples come over early Sunday afternoon to meet me. Cheese and crackers, wine, drinks if anyone wanted one. I was only too glad to help. I set out the bottles of liquor and made drinks for the guests as they came in. About an hour along I spied Robin talking with one of her friends, a distinguished-looking gentleman with salt-and-pepper hair, and, seeing their glasses were nearly empty, I went up and asked them both if they would like a refill.

After I made the drinks and brought them over, Robin took me aside. "George, I appreciate your help, but if I'd wanted a bartender I'd have hired one," she told me quietly. "I want people to get to know you and what a wonderful man you are and you're not giving them the chance. Instead of mixing people drinks, from now on just mix."

That was all I needed. With Cynnie I'd always made drinks for the entire party and really didn't talk to anyone for any length of time; certainly I didn't sit down with an attractive woman and have a good conversation with her. It wasn't how we'd done things. But I saw what Robin was saying and understood why she was saying it. It was really quite exhilarating to feel free in a social situation. I kissed Robin on the forehead and started up a conversation with a lovely woman named Joyce that lasted for almost an hour, then with a Chicago businessman and then with another woman. When everyone finally left, Robin told me I was wonderful, the hit of the party, and she thanked me.

"I'm a quick learner," I said.

Was it unfair for me to ask Robin to leave Chicago for Greene, New York? I can see where some people might say so, might even think that the last thing Robin needed was to get married again. Furthermore, she had an active career in Chicago as a photographer, lots of good friends in the city and suburbs, and a beautiful apartment in an exciting and cultural metropolis. And I wanted her to relocate, emotionally and physically, in a small New York town in the Southern Tier?

Yes. I understood all that she'd be giving up but I refused to let it dissuade me, because I knew Robin would have an even better life with me, as my wife, in Greene. I was determined that she look only on the bright side and not even consider the question of what she would be leaving behind. God put eyes in the front of our head for a reason, I told her. So we could see ahead, to the future. And ours would be a bright one.

When I got home from that weekend I thought long and hard and then sat down and wrote her a three-page letter, giving her twelve reasons why she should marry me and also listing the qualities I was looking for in a woman, all of which she had in abundance. Intelligence, warmth, humor, sex appeal, character, looks, spirituality, family values, creativity. When we spoke during the week, after she'd read the letter, she told me how moved she was by it, how touched that I held her in such high esteem. But she hadn't changed her mind.

In June of 1978 I took Robin to the annual trade show of the material-handling industry, which was held in Detroit. I introduced her to a number of my friends of many years standing. They loved her and she seemed genuinely to like them. When I walked her to the gate for her flight back to Chicago, I brought up, yet again, the subject of marriage.

She asked me what was wrong with the way things were, the great time we were having. Nothing at all, I said, but something is missing when you go through life without real commitment, the commitment of marriage. After she'd boarded her flight, I went to the Admirals Club and wrote her my most heartfelt letter yet. And probably my shortest. What I told her, in essence, was this: *Just as money without working for it is empty, love without commitment is hollow.*

Robin told me later that when she got my letter her heart started racing and she thought: This guy is *really* serious. I can't play games any longer. She also said my use of the word "commitment," at the airport in Detroit and again in my letter, had hit home powerfully.

But still she wasn't ready.

A lot was happening in Robin's life at that time. First, there was Bill, the lawyer and special friend of long standing. Something had happened, because he was no longer the major obstacle I had always thought of him as; he was no longer the "other man." One of Robin's great virtues is her honesty, her openness. I knew, because Robin told me, that Bill was still very important to her. But neither one of them wanted to get married again. He felt he was too old for her, seventeen years her senior, and she really didn't want to give up her freedom. In whatever way all that added up, their relationship began to drift. Was it also because a certain George G. Raymond Jr. wanted nothing more than to marry her? That possibility certainly crossed my mind.

But her former lover the lawyer, as it developed, wasn't the main reason why Robin wasn't jumping at the opportunity to meet me at the altar. The main reason was the "other" Bill in her life, her ex-husband, Bill Ylvisaker.

When she had signed the divorce papers, she had said goodbye to him legally, but saying goodbye to him emotionally was something else. She was holding on. She had built a new life on the still smoldering ashes of her first marriage, and had no intention of putting herself in harm's way again. That was the crux of it. She started seeing a therapist, whom she soon came to trust completely.

One day, in a session, after the therapist had come to realize that George Raymond would send the Marines for Robin if necessary, he said, in addressing her hesitation, "I want you to close your eyes and conjure up a picture of Bill Y. and say goodbye to him."

"Goodbye, Bill," she said without energy.

But it wasn't convincing. He pressed her. "Come on, Robin. Remember the first time Bill told you about Jane, the English girl he'd met on a plane crossing the Channel? Shortly afterwards he said he wanted a divorce. Do you remember all that?"

Robin pinched her eyes tightly closed. "Yes."

"And the anguish you suffered for months afterward because of the breakup of your family?"

"Yes."

"Now, say goodbye to that son-of-a-bitch. And say it out loud. Not once but three times. And keep your eyes closed until you're finished."

She struggled. She must have struggled mightily to finally admit that her marriage to Bill Y. was over. To admit he had a new life without her. And to realize she could have a new and full life without him. And, when she thought of the pain he had put her through, a far better one.

"Goodbye, Bill," she said, the words coming from the innermost place in her heart. "Goodbye, goodbye."

Robin raced home and called me immediately. "George, the answer is yes. I'll marry you!"

I could hardly speak, I was so overcome with joy. I managed to say, "When?"

"Soon. This fall."

As the wedding approached, I called Robin and offered to come to Chicago and pick her up. But she said, "No, George. This is something I want to do myself. I have to decide what to take and what not to. There's just so much."

"Get a pad of paper," I said, "and list all the things with special memories, and then prioritize the list until you have it pared down to a dozen things. Then take those twelve things—and don't look back."

Whether she followed my advice precisely, I don't know. But she told me it helped. Anyway, we were planning to keep her Chicago apartment, so the items she couldn't take to Greene wouldn't be lost and forgotten.

A day later she called me, her voice filled with worry.

"Robin, what's wrong?"

"I'm getting cold feet."

My heart sank. "About marrying me?"

"No, no, I love you, George." She gave a little laugh. "About moving to Greene. Last night I stood at my window looking at the city lights and then out at Lake Michigan and thinking, How can I leave this wonderful city, my home, and go live in a one-horse town of 2,000 people? Will I fit? I'm serious, darling. I'm an outsider, coming in with different clothes, different attitudes, different everything."

"Robin, sweetheart—"

"Not only that," she said, "the thought of living in your house, the house where you and Cynnie lived, frightens me. I don't know if I can do it."

"Robin," I said, "in the first place you're not an outsider. You could step into any room in the world and fit in. As far as the house, do you know the story of the wren?"

"No," she said.

"Well, when wrens pair up it's for life, and in the spring when they go back up north, the male goes ahead of the female, and he looks for a place to raise a family. First he finds food, then he spots a possible wren house. And if it's a nest that's been used before, he cleans it up and then fills it with twigs, twigs only. When that chore is done he comes out on the 'stoop' and sings a beautiful song. His 'wife' hears it, and flies right over. But when she inspects the place, it's never to her liking, and she throws out every single twig and builds her own nest. That's my promise to you, Robin. With the Greene house, if you're not happy in it you can rebuild it from scratch."

Three days before the wedding—the official day was October 14—I sent a car to pick up Robin's mother in Woodstock, N.Y. Robin had called her and asked her to bake an apple pie in "George's kitchen," so that when Robin and I got to the house from the airport, it would smell like home. Sure enough, when I carried Robin across the threshold—I was jumping the gun on this, admittedly— Robin's mother was there to welcome us, a wonderful aroma of apples and cinnamon filling the house.

The only aspect of the wedding, or pre-wedding, that caused me any stress was my relationship with my children. It wasn't what a father, marrying a second time, hoped it would be. A couple of days before the big event we all had lunch together, and there was a good bit of negativism in the air. Pete, Steve and Jean seemed to have a stone wall around them and I wasn't getting through, maybe because they weren't letting me through. It wasn't a happy lunch. Finally I said, "If you can't come to this wedding and smile and be pleasant, then don't come. This is a joyous time in my life and nothing in the world will stand between me and Robin and our life together."

They knew I was totally serious, but I can't say, as we walked out of the restaurant, that they were any happier. Was I getting married too soon after the death of their mother? Now that I was taking on a new wife, were they worried about their role, their place, in the family? It was never spoken; all I got was a general displeasure from my kids as to what was happening. I was sorry about it but what could I do? As I drove home, I thought, Every cloud has a silver lining, yes; but even the brightest cloud has traces of gray.

On the Friday morning before our wedding the next day, as I was puttering around in the kitchen, Robin's mother came in and asked me what I was doing. I said, "Making your daughter's breakfast. So she can have it in bed."

"This I have to see." Gertrude had come to America from her native Germany in 1923, and you could still detect a faint and charming accent in her speech. In her marriage to Robin's father, he always came first.

Ten minutes later, when she came in and saw Robin with a breakfast tray on her lap—orange juice, coffee, scrambled eggs and toast—she shook her head in wonderment. "Good Lord," she exclaimed, "the Kaiser never had it so good!"

We were married on October 14th of that year, 1978, by the Rev. David Robinson in Zion Episcopal Church in Greene. Robin's son, Billy, gave her away. In attendance, from my side, were my sons, Pete and Steve, Steve's wife, Beth, and my daughter, Jean, who had taken a place of her own soon after the trial ended. On Robin's side were her mother, sister Hala and her husband David Lawrence, and her brother Tony. Also Robin's children, Laurie, Beth, Billy, and Amy. It was a beautiful ceremony and the reception, at the house, was a truly splendid family affair. Champagne flowed, and everyone made toasts. My new brother-in-law, Tony, said he was worried that I'd renege on my gift to all the male members of the wedding party, because of all the expenses I was footing for this weekend of weekends. "Well, you'd better not," Tony said, looking right at me, "because I want my fork-lift truck!"

So started my married life with Robin. One of the first things I did was instruct my trainer to start selling all thirty-two of my Morgan horses. My time and energy were now fully taken up with marriage and my life with Robin. She didn't play the part of the female wren 100 percent, but she did quite a bit, nevertheless, toward change—shifting furniture about, hanging new paintings, organizing the kitchen to her own liking. I couldn't really tell if she was happy in the house where Cynnie had lived, but always game and always the worker, she was trying to make the house hers. Our first year in Greene was the happiest of my life to that point. I loved coming home to Robin, to find a fire going, something delicious simmering on the stove. Then one day I walked in and the house was empty.

"Robin?"

No answer. Louder. "Robin, are you here?"

Silence.

My thoughts rushed back to that afternoon in June, now over two years ago. Where was she? I began to panic, searched every room in the house. Coming up from the basement, still calling her name, I rushed outside... and saw her footsteps in the falling snow leading into the woods. I followed her tracks, now really frightened; and there she was, walking toward me, cheeks ruddy, looking beautiful and wonderfully alive. I rushed out to her, took her in my arms. She knew I loved her, but this was a bit much.

"George, my goodness!"

I explained to her what I'd just been through and told her never, under any circumstances, to leave the house again, if I wasn't home, without leaving me a note.

"But I only went for a thirty-minute walk up in the woods!"

No difference. Unless she enjoyed putting me through hell, she should leave me a note. She apologized, promised me she would, and she still does it to this day. We walked inside together. Perhaps I had overreacted, but I couldn't help it. Once traumatized, always frightened.

For all her changes and re-stylings, the house wasn't coming together for Robin, she confessed to me in the fall of 1980; after two years she still didn't feel it was right for us. So we decided to do a major rebuild. Add here, tear down there. We brought in architects, contractors; but the more plans we saw, the more we talked, the more we realized it wasn't going to work.

Shortly before Christmas of that year, at dinner in Binghamton with friends—two of whom happened to be partners in a real estate office there—Robin mentioned that our plans to add on to the house in Greene hadn't worked out. On hearing that, one of the women said, "Why don't you move to Binghamton?"

I said, quite seriously, "Do you have anything to show us?"

"Do we ever!" said both women at once.

That night, when we got home, Robin and I talked long and hard about where we might want to live. We decided we had five options. We could: 1) Stay in Greene; 2) Move to Binghamton, twenty miles to the south; 3) Move to Norwich, twenty miles north; 4) Move to Ithaca, fifty miles away; or 5) We could move to Chicago and I could commute, something I'd done while we were courting.

Our first step was to explore Option Binghamton. Robin called Nancy, one of the real estate partners. "You said you had places to show us. Can we come by today?"

"Sure!"

Nancy gave us directions to her house on Riverside Drive, overlooking the Susquehanna River. As we drove down Riverside Drive, we saw a big empty lot, and I said, "I bet that's the parcel she'll try to sell us." It looked barren and cold, not a tree on it, and both of us said together, "No way!"

When we got there, Nancy said, "I want to show you something. It's the last lot on Riverside Drive. But you have to follow me, on foot, down to the river. I want to show you something special."

Of course it was the same lot, but looking at it from a different angle made its three acres appear much warmer, more attractive. Its potential, for the place of a beautiful new home, was fabulous. Nancy showed us a number of houses that day, but none of them really interested us. Finally, I asked her the price of the empty lot on the river, and the figure she gave us was ridiculously high. We thanked her for the tour and drove home to Greene.

After a talk that did not last particularly long, Robin and I looked at one another and admitted that we wanted to live in Binghamton, on the property with a view of the Susquehanna River!

We called Nancy and offered half of the asking price. There was, of course, bargaining that took several days, and although we did not get the lot for half, we did get what we thought was a good deal. And so we went ahead and spent all the money we'd saved—and then some—on building our dream house.

When it was done, we were both very happy and excited. Robin had her own nest at last. And I? I had a new and beautiful place to call home; but more important by far, as we walked in hand in hand, I would be living in it with the woman I loved.

11

A Different World

ack in 1980, when Dick Beckhard was teaching at MIT, he realized that very little was known about family firms as an area of study. At that time 95 percent of all the businesses in the world were family-owned and -controlled firms, and Dick recognized that business schools "didn't teach a damn thing about them." So he put together a research project, making sure that it was multinational and "multi-role"—the latter meaning that it involved people who represented such categories as the founder of a company, the son or daughter of the founder, the brother of the founder, etc. He then came to me and asked if the Raymond Foundation would support a three-year research project, in cooperation with the leaders of seven other family-owned companies.

A number of family firms that Dick had advised as a consultant agreed to participate in a study to determine what research existed in the field; they found there was practically nothing. A year later this group held a meeting at Endicott House at MIT to discuss important areas of potential study, such as succession planning and bringing family members into the business. That process worked so well that the participants wanted a second meeting the following year, and then a third. Finally they realized that it would benefit everyone to have a formal organization.

Dick figured it would take approximately $10,000 to get started, so he, his wife and Barbara Hollander, a family and organization consultant, each put up $2,000. Then they sent out letters of recruitment to a handful of other people. Robin and I went to the first meeting, paid $2,000 apiece, and became members of the founding board. That was how the Family Firm Institute started in Dick Beckhard's Manhattan living room.

At our first official conference, about two years later, we produced a document that described FFI. Here are excerpts of that report:

THE FAMILY FIRM INSTITUTE

RATIONALE

Family business is the predominant form of business in the Western world. Ninety percent of all businesses including corporations, partnerships, and sole-proprietorships are family owned or family controlled.

Family firms produce one half of the GNP and employ half the nation's work force. They range in size from the Mom and Pop store to Bechtel and the far-flung Marmon enterprises. The contribution of family firms to the economy is significant, yet the survival rate is low. Only 30 percent make it to the second generation. Family businesses encounter problems such as conflicts over succession issues, sibling rivalry, inability to keep competent non-family personnel, management of family shareholders, and complex estate planning.

Until recently, very little literature and research focused on the problems of family business. In the past five years, interest and activity have expanded. Business schools are recognizing that the family firm has unique characteristics that cannot be addressed by traditional management processes. Decreased career options in the public sector, the decline of heavy industry, the dramatic rise in entrepreneurship, and the success of the Japanese in creating family type approaches to management have all served to heighten awareness of the importance of the family firm. Research, writing, and consultation to family firms has increased, and family firm members have been responsive to opportunities for education and training.

In response to the importance of family business, a field of knowledge is developing which draws its information from various areas including management theory, family theory, finance, accounting, law, and government. What is needed to further the development of this field is an umbrella organization that will bring together individuals and organizations who are working toward ways to insure continuity for family firms. Toward this end, the Family Firm Institute has been formed.

MISSION

The Family Firm Institute is an independent, multi-disciplinary organization formed in response to the vital societal significance of family owned businesses. Its purpose is to contribute to the understanding of family business and to enhance the ability to manage such businesses effectively. The Institute will stimulate, generate, and disseminate knowledge and promote communication and collaboration among individuals and organizations involved in family businesses.

FOUNDING BOARD

RICHARD BECKHARD, Richard Beckhard Associates, retired adjunct professor of management and organization behavior, Alfred P. Sloan School of Management, MIT;

BARBARA S. HOLLANDER, PH.D., family and organization consultant;

ELAINE KEPNER, PH.D., Gestalt Institute; Fielding Institute, partner, Richard Beckhard Associates;

IVAN S. LANSBERG, PH.D., assistant professor of organization behavior, Yale School of Organization & Management;

AARON LEVINSON, retired Chairman of the Board and Chief Executive Officer, Levinson Steel Company;

GEORGE RAYMOND, JR., Chairman, The Raymond Corporation;

ROBIN RAYMOND, Professional Portrait Photographer.

The following is an example of some of the research and writing done by FFI members, in this case one of its founders.

THE SEVEN SIDES OF CONFLICT
IN THE FAMILY BUSINESS

IVAN LANSBERG JR.

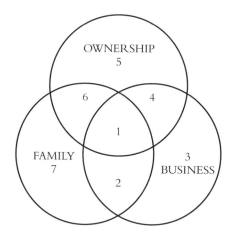

Sometimes a picture is worth a thousand words. The above diagram, first developed by John Davis and Renato Taguiri at Harvard, gives us a useful way of understanding many of the conflicts that arise in family firms. This framework assumes that individuals located in the family business, and ownership circles, have a unique set of needs and expectations towards the family business. Typically, people in family businesses perceive conflict as resulting from personality differences only (such as, "If only Dad wouldn't be this way... we wouldn't have a problem here"). In contrast, this framework assumes that "Dad's views" are determined to a greater extent by the position he holds in the family business than by his personality. Summarized below are some of the key concerns that arise from each of the seven positions making up a family business.

POSITION #1: (IN BUSINESS, IN OWNERSHIP AND IN THE FAMILY) This position is usually occupied by the principal owner-manager or founder and his or her successor-to-be. It is the toughest position to have in a family business since it requires the constant mediation of conflicting demands: Family members who want to be looked after and assured that the business will help them attain their personal goals and aspirations; stock holders who expect good business performance and a substantial return on their equity; and others involved in the management of the company who expect a high degree of managerial leadership and professionalism. Individuals in this position have their careers tied to the business and they often feel that their personal success depends on the success of the business. They frequently believe that family members not working in the business are an obstacle to attaining business goals. Finally, since this also happens to be the most influential position in the family business, it often brings envy from others.

POSITION #2: (OUT OF OWNERSHIP, IN BUSINESS AND IN FAMILY) This position is often occupied by members of the owner-manager's family such as his or her sons and daughters, as well as members of his or her extended family. Family members in the business are usually viewed in one of two ways: they are either "high performers" or "poor performers." In a family company, the assessment of performance is affected by family dynamics and is therefore a matter of opinion. "High performing" relatives are among the most valued employees in a family business. They frequently are very loyal, have technical backgrounds and occupy sensitive positions (such as chief financial officer) in which their family connection to the owner-manager affords them a high degree of trust. "High performing" relatives are often mediators between the family and the non-family employees. They often look forward to the day when they will acquire some stock. The acquisition of stock is often of great symbolic value since it signals a strong commitment to these individuals. "Poor performing" relatives are often placed in menial jobs where they cannot do too much harm. These individuals are often the scapegoats of the system and, as a result, frequently suffer low self-esteem.

POSITION #3: (IN BUSINESS, OUT OF OWNERSHIP AND OUT OF FAMILY) These are the senior non-family managers who are responsible for the success of the business. Good performers are often concerned about whether top positions in the company are reserved for family members only. "Old timers" in this position are often very close and loyal to the owner-manager and feel like "adopted" members of the family. On the other hand, "newcomers," frequently armed with MBAs, struggle to understand the family's culture and often resent the use of family criteria in making business decisions. Individuals in this position tend to play an important role in the training of family members and are often upset when the family members that they trained are promoted to positions above them.

POSITION #4: (IN BUSINESS, IN OWNERSHIP AND OUT OF FAMILY) Typically, these are either "old timers" who have been rewarded with stock ownership by the owner-manager or "newcomers" who acquired some stock as part of their entry contract. For the "old timers," stock ownership demonstrates that they are appreciated by the family and reinforces their loyalty to the owner-manager. For "newcomers," stock ownership guarantees that they will be able to influence decisions without greatly jeopardizing their jobs. Individuals in this position are often concerned about the additional benefits and stature that their stock ownership gives them relative to non-family employees who do not have any stock. Typically, stock ownership carries with it the expectation of more involvement in strategic decisions as well as more perks.

POSITION #5: (OUT OF BUSINESS, OUT OF FAMILY BUT IN OWNERSHIP) These individuals are essentially outside investors, typically friends of the owner-manager, who believe in his or her competence and are willing to invest their money in his or her company. Their chief concern is making sure that the company is well managed so that their investment is protected. They are usually very concerned about receiving good dividends and are members of a board of directors in those rare cases when a board of directors exists.

POSITION #6: (IN FAMILY, IN OWNERSHIP AND OUT OF BUSINESS) This position includes the owner-manager's spouse as well as his or her children who have inherited stock in the company. These people are often concerned with inclusion and fairness. Their concerns over inclusion stem from the fact that those who do not work in the business have difficulties connecting with those that do. They often feel that those who do not work in the business are not full members of the family. This is evident during family gatherings when those who do not work in the business cannot participate in important family conversations about the business. The concern over fairness comes from the fact that these individuals are often "rich on paper but poor on cash". Owning stock in a family company can be a frustrating experience since the free use of ones assets are impossible. Often, people in this position resort to "tapping" the business for resources in an effort to "get something" for their ownership; this includes the use of company cars as well as relying on the company's clerical staff.

POSITION #7: (OUT OF BUSINESS, OUT OF OWNERSHIP BUT IN FAMILY) This position is typically occupied by members of the extended family. These individuals often envy the comparative wealth of the owner-manager's core family. When these individuals are not welcome to work in the business, they often harbor a feeling of being excluded. If, on the other hand, they chose not to join the family business, they often feel that they have "abandoned" the family in pursuit of their own interests.

So what is the practical value of this framework? First, it shows that differences of opinion are inevitable in a family business; they are built into the structure of the system. Second, it heightens our awareness of the perspectives that come with each position and proposes that understanding these various perspectives is an important ingredient in learning to manage a family business effectively. Third, and most important, it focuses our attention away from blaming and trying to change people's personalities and onto developing constructive ways of managing conflicts that inevitably arise.

FFI spent the first few years of its existence recruiting members, building its program, and generally refining the concept of the organization. In the middle of this developmental period, Dick Beckhard was invited to Switzerland by a former client, Ivan Lansberg Sr. (our colleague's father), to evaluate the curriculum of the International Management Institute which the Nestle Corporation originally started for training its own management and later opened to other businesses. Once there he took it upon himself to broach the subject of family businesses to Lansberg, IMI's former chairman. Would IMI be interested, Dick asked, in adding the study of family businesses to its broad and diversified curriculum?

As he was to find out, the IMI faculty had no enthusiasm for the idea. Luckily, one of the people attending that meeting was Stephan Schmidheime, a wealthy Swiss businessman who was IMI's current chairman, and owner of a family business, and he thought it was a great idea. With his encouragement and financial help, IMI set up an "executive in residence" position. Whoever held this post would have the responsibility of administering the program: the organizing and

running of classes on family business to interested groups and individuals. To my knowledge, this was the first time that any institution
of higher learning had ever offered courses on the subject.

At the first FFI conference, held in Boston in 1988, the chairman
of the action committee asked if anyone in attendance might like to
spend a year in Geneva, Switzerland, as the Executive in Residence at
the International Management Institute. As an ex-GI, well-trained in
the practice of never volunteering, I totally surprised myself by raising my hand .

The current FFI executive was halfway through his stint. I would
be leaving in six months, but it was suggested that I make a trial run:
go to Geneva beforehand, see what I thought, then decide if I still
wanted the job. When the meeting ended I immediately called
Robin.

Not wasting any time, I asked her how she would like to spend a
year in Switzerland.

She answered, "When do we leave?"

As suggested, we caught a flight to Geneva for a "look see," attending the week-long seminar given by the man currently the Executive
in Residence. Robin and I were supposed to be observers, but when
the group began a role-playing demonstration, we knew it wouldn't
be long, given our experience in "truth dramas," before we were
active participants.

John Ward, a professor of business at Loyola University in Chicago,
was conducting the demonstration. For one scenario, he chose a man
and a woman to play a brother and sister who were the owners of a
family business (operated by the brother) faced with the problem of
the sister's request that he employ her spoiled, difficult son. To play the
man's role, Ward chose an uptight, or at the least formal, Irish businessman, and to play the sister's role he selected the only woman in
the class, Robin.

She immersed herself in the plot, giving the Irishman a hard time for refusing to hire her "son." At one point, truly exasperated, Robin cried out, "It's not fair, and I'm pissed. You've got *your* son in the business. Our late father started this company, not you. I'm really angry with you, Sean, and I'm going to talk to *mother!*" Robin's outburst cracked the tension of the thirty CEOs from different European countries, and they all broke into spontaneous laughter, recognizing the universality of problems in family businesses.

Robin's "brother" came right back at her, obviously upset, and they continued venting for another few minutes before John Ward stepped in, something like a referee, to signal the end of the role playing. During the break, the Irish businessman told Robin he wasn't upset with *her;* it wasn't personal. The role-playing had simply hit home, and he was grateful to Robin for helping him "see" what his problems truly were with regard to his own family life and business. Soon others began telling similar stories about their lives and careers, and I realized that a major breakthrough had occurred, thanks to Robin. It turned out to be a fabulous seminar with people realizing that everyone's family and business problems were really all the same. When it was all over, Robin and I decided to take the job and come to Geneva in the fall.

When we got there in September of 1989, I thought I would be greeted with open arms by fellow faculty members and warmly embraced by the director. Instead, I was totally ignored. By everybody—except June Lossius, a woman assigned to offer me whatever secretarial and other help I might need.

After I'd been at the school for ten days, I asked June, the widow of an American businessman who had run the Industrial Conference Board, a worldwide business organization throughout Europe, if there was some kind of inter-faculty communication system.

"Yes," she said. "Why?"

"Because I'd like to let people know I'm here!"

With her help, I disseminated the information as to who I was and why I was at IMI. In response, I got exactly one phone call. A fellow faculty member named Pierre called to say, "Sorry about your treatment. Every colleague, both at IMI and IMEDA, should call you or write you a letter; but they won't. Welcome aboard anyway!"

Pierre turned out to be a charming, witty fellow. He clued me in on the fierce academic infighting between the two institutions, which were in the process of merging and moving to the new IMEDA campus in Lausanne. There was a certain irony involved: IMI and IMEDA taught their graduate students how to handle mergers and acquisitions but, clearly, they were struggling in the actual hands-on process of doing it themselves.

Later that fall my new friend informed me that the director of IMI, to my amazement and concern, was lukewarm toward the existence of a school of business in general and my seminar in particular. Needless to say, I was nervous as to my chances of success without his support. A bit disillusioned, I pushed ahead with my plans.

My first weeklong session was scheduled for December, and I had worked hard to make sure I would have enough participants. I ended up with twenty CEOs of family businesses from almost every country in Europe, which meant the school made a good deal of money, more money than any other program offered by the school. To say the least, the administration, notably the director, was impressed and very happy. I was off to a great start.

During my first six months in Geneva I contacted a great number of people involved with family firms in various countries, told them about FFI, and asked if they would like to join. They were definitely interested, so, paying my own way, I flew back to America to attend a Family Firm Institute meeting to propose the formation of a European arm to the organization. To my surprise, the response was

"No." Disappointed by FFI's response, I returned to Europe and did a good deal of thinking.

From the beginning, it had always been my desire to see the Family Firm Institute set up to help members of family businesses deal with common problems. Instead, it became a quasi-trade organization for those who *helped* family businesses, the so-called suppliers to family businesses, such as academic behaviorists, consultants, even lawyers and accountants.

I didn't find fault with my fellow founders of FFI, but I did take issue with their idea of what the nature of the organization should be. Because of that, and because FFI had rejected my plan on my recent visit, I set about to create a new organization in Europe, namely Family Business Network, as a "distant cousin" of FFI in North America. (At the risk of sounding immodest, I have to mention that FBN is now many times larger than FFI in the United States. In fact, the Family Business Network is today a worldwide organization, while the Family Firm Institute has very few if any members outside of North America.)

From time to time my son Steve would call me in Geneva from California, where he was running an automated canning business we had bought, the Wiebe Corp. He was ready to come home, to Greene, New York, to play an important part in The Raymond Corporation—in other words, to head it. He was angry that I wasn't doing anything to facilitate his promotion. Ross Colquhoun, president of The Raymond Corporation kept telling Steve that he would be the next president. Who else? The building had his name on it! As for my feelings, I still didn't feel Steve was quite ready to run the company. I felt he needed to manage a Raymond dealership to finish his training for the presidency. In a couple of more years, when Ross stepped down, Steve would then have the experience and maturity to handle the top job. True, he was already forty, and I had taken over as president at thirty-three; but there was a world of difference between running a small family-owned foundry and a growing, international corporation. I told Steve to be patient, but I'm not sure he listened.

As an indication of how well my tour at IMD (International Managerial Development, the name given the merger of IMI and EMEDA) worked out, when it was over the administration asked me to come back for another year. They even offered to pay my expenses, which they hadn't done before. I must admit that I was sorely tempted, but Robin had just left for America to arrange for her daughter Amy's wedding, and I had all our personal belongings boxed and ready for shipping. I declined his offer.

Before I left, the director asked me if I had any suggestions as to who should be the first to occupy the Chair in Family Business at IMD. Quietly honored that he had sought my opinion, I mentioned the name Alden Lank, a Canadian by birth who had been educated at Middlebury College and Harvard Business School. During my year in Switzerland, Lank had worked tirelessly to learn the ins and outs of family business. He got the job and proved more than able. On the strength of his work and my recommendation, IMD granted him tenure. He taught until his retirement, at which point he assumed the leadership of FBN.

While in Geneva I realized something about myself I never had before—how much I enjoyed focusing on a single task. In a corporate environment an executive is constantly pulled in many directions. He (or she) often feels fragmented, even torn. During my year in Switzerland, I'd directed my energy toward exactly what I wanted to do—administer and teach family-business courses, as well as organize a network for family-run businesses in Europe.

As I sat on the plane that would take me home, I began reviewing my year abroad. I had accomplished my purpose as Executive in Residence at IMD, and I had built a new self-supporting program at the school. Furthermore, I had been instrumental in starting a European-based family business network, FBN. All in all it was a very successful tour of duty, but a year abroad had been enough and I was eagerly looking forward to returning to The Raymond Corporation.

As my jet flew over the snow-topped Alps, heading west, I was happy to be going home, and also happy in the knowledge that I had just had one of the most rewarding and fulfilling years of my life.

12

Betrayal and Turnabout

The Switzerland sojourn over, June 1990, I got back to business at The Raymond Corporation, where I had stepped down as CEO and taken the job of Chairman of the Board. To review the bidding:

My first two choices to succeed me as chief executive hadn't worked out. Jim Hardy, given power, wasn't satisfied simply to run Raymond. He wanted to own 51 percent of it! But his attempt to buy out shareholders and make the company *his,* didn't fly. It took a nosedive and he became a smoldering casualty of his own greed and arrogance.

Then came Bill Weber. At times I think back to my retirement party in 1987, when I said, "If Raymond can become a 200-million-dollar, then a 300-million-dollar, then a 500-million-dollar company, William R. Weber is the executive who will make it happen." I reflect on that evening at the Binghamton City Club, and can only shake my head. Weber made nothing happen, except that overnight he became dictatorial and destroyed company morale—not something for an executive to put on his resume.

But I had a good man at the helm now. During the early and mid-1990s Ross Colquhoun had done a great job; in his first five years he had brought Raymond from the doldrums to the brink of the twenty-first century with a greatly improved sales force, a first-class engineering performance, and what was considered the most competitive manufacturing organization in the lift-truck world. I had complete faith in Ross; his loyalty to the company and to me appeared unquestionable.

One day in 1994 Robin and I raised the question, as we were talking at the breakfast table: Who would act on my behalf on the Raymond board if I should become seriously ill, in some way incapacitated? I was seventy-three, and it seemed a fair inquiry. After some discussion, I decided on Gail Webster: we should name her to the board of directors.

Gail had started her banking career in Binghamton with Marine Midland's trust department, where she had succeeded the man who, acting on my father's instructions, had set up ten trusts, each one containing Raymond stock, for my father's grandchildren—my sister's seven kids and my three. My sister had chosen Gail to act as trustee of her own assets. I also had my money with Gail, who was co-trustee with my sister and me of my father's estate, my mother's estate and, finally, the estate of my first wife, Cynthia. I could think of no one better qualified or suited to represent me on the Raymond board than Gail Webster, since she had been our trust officer for thirty years.

As chairman of the board, I didn't have to go through Ross, but as a courtesy to the company's chief executive I did, giving him the rationale behind my request. He listened attentively, understood, and seemed agreeable.

I was very fond of Ross Colquhoun. We were close personal friends, for one thing. He often came to Florida to visit Robin and me in our Naples home, where we had moved after I retired. We would play golf and talk about the future of the company and generally have a good, relaxed time. Once Gail's name became a topic, Ross would always ask if we could invite her for the evening—at that point she was president of the Naples branch of Huntington National Bank. He seemed to really enjoy her company and obviously wanted to get to know her as a future member of the board.

It was a good time at Raymond. We were growing, our numbers were excellent, workers were taking home healthy paychecks. The only thing not sitting well with me was the value of our stock. Ross agreed that $16 was low but he wasn't concerned. One of these quarters Wall Street would get the word that we were an aggressive, innovative company, and our prices would take off. We would also start paying dividends again. When, Ross wouldn't say. He would hold off until the company reached the level of profitability it needed to begin paying shareholders. Certainly by next year. But when "next year" came, it was the same story.

Personally, my own income was suffering, but I was always one to believe that the company's health came first. I have to admit, sometimes I wondered if the "company's health" was what motivated Ross. I didn't see him that often, and he could have reasons I didn't know about for maintaining the moratorium. But I didn't dwell on it. As a company we were going great guns.

With mandatory retirement age for Raymond employees set at sixty-five, Ross wouldn't be running the show too much longer. Wanting to guarantee Ross a place in the company when a new chief executive took over—Steve, now a mature and tested forty-six, might be getting his chance at last—I decided in 1995, at a board meeting at Bolton Landing on Lake Champlain, to step down as chairman and give the title to Ross. He would also stay on as chief executive.

I was so choked up I could hardly get the words out to make the announcement. I had retired once before, when Bill Weber had taken over as president, but stepping aside as president of a family-controlled company is different from stepping down as chairman. In the former, you give up executive power but you're still a strong player; in the latter, you're all but hanging up your cleats. I would stay on the Raymond board, but the play-calling and scrimmaging I had done for fifty years was ending. I would have a place on the bench.

I bled that afternoon on the shores of Lake Champlain, and I'll tell the world I bled orange.

Gail Webster made numerous trips around the country, some in the dead of winter, to coincide with board (and annual) meetings, largely because I wanted her to show Ross and others that she was committed to becoming a director. All of us—Robin and I, Ross, Gail, sometimes another board member and his wife—would go out to dinner on these occasions. Ross would tell jokes and generally dominate the conversation. There was very little "getting-to-know-Gail" involved, as far as I could see.

I began to have doubts, *new* doubts about the chairman. Was he talking out of both sides of his mouth, pretending to like Gail, agreeing with me that she would be a wonderful addition to the board, when secretly he had no intentions of taking her on? I didn't know. But then I thought, Stop worrying. It's no problem. She'll be elected.

The board met at the Breakers Hotel in Palm Beach in early 1996, and I planned on bringing up Gail's name for a vote.

Ross, knowing that I would almost certainly be doing this, sent a letter to each member of the board, enclosing three legal opinions, two declaring possible conflicts of interest if Gail were elected. Namely, she was the president of a bank that also acted as a fiduciary for a majority stock interest—meaning me. Now I was really feeling suspicious. I attended a meeting of the board's Human Resources Committee on Friday, March 1. After I'd asked just a few questions, it became clear to me that Gail's prospects were in serious jeopardy. Especially when Ross, who was a member of the Human Resources Committee, declared he would oppose Gail Webster's election to the

Raymond board—and added that if she were elected, he would resign from the company!

Stunned, I did a mental vote count, and realized that the Human Resources Committee—and therefore the full board—would support Ross. It would be pointless to even put Gail's name up. With that, the truth hit me. I had given Ross the chairmanship, and with the total power he now had, he was cutting me out. In less than a year's time, he had turned *my* board into *his* board. Should Gail Webster be elected for the purpose of watching after *George Raymond's* interests? Ross Colquhoun didn't think so. He had total power now and he wasn't going to risk or endanger it.

I left the meeting, went to my room, and without even bothering to turn on the light, sat there thinking about what had just happened.

I concentrated particularly on what had always been my personal financial objectives and how they would be affected by this sudden and unexpected turn of events. Eventually, in the dim light, I scribbled my thoughts down on paper. On a sheet of hotel stationery, in large block letters, I printed the following:

I BELIEVED BEFORE *THE HUMAN RESOURCES COMMITTEE MEETING:*

1. WHAT WAS GOOD FOR THE COMPANY WAS CONSIDERED GOOD FOR GEORGE RAYMOND AND THE RAYMOND FAMILY.

2. ANY SHORT TERM SACRIFICE NECESSARY WOULD BE TAKEN FOR THE GOOD OF THE COMPANY, IF THE LONG-TERM PROSPECT IS TO STRENGTHEN THE COMPANY.

3. ANY PERSONAL ACTIONS MAY BE TAKEN ONLY AFTER CONSIDERING THE EFFECT ON THE COMPANY AND SECONDARILY WHAT BENEFIT IT IS TO GEORGE RAYMOND AND THE RAYMOND FAMILY.

I BELIEVE AFTER *THE HUMAN RESOURCES COMMITTEE MEETING:*

1. ACTIONS GOOD FOR GEORGE RAYMOND AND THE RAYMOND FAMILY MAY NOT BE IN THE BEST INTEREST OF THE COMPANY MANAGEMENT.

2. GEORGE RAYMOND MUST NOW LOOK AT THE SHORT TERM AND THIS MAY NOT BE IN THE BEST INTEREST OF THE COMPANY MANAGEMENT.

3. THE HEALTH AND SAFETY OF GEORGE RAYMOND AND HIS FAMILY'S INVESTMENT MUST BE CONSIDERED FIRST IN MAKING FINANCIAL DECISIONS.

The next morning I went to the meeting of the full board. I had told the chairman of the Human Resources Committee I had an addendum I wanted to make after his report. He finished up but "forgot" to mention my request, so I stood up and made it anyway.

My addendum consisted of the statement I had written out the day before in my room. When the directors heard me say, "It always used to be company first and family second, but from now on it's going to be the other way around," their reaction was a shocked silence. They knew the world of The Raymond Corporation had just changed, radically and fundamentally. They also knew that I had just declared war.

For decades, I had been exhorting, urging, and bullying everyone in the family to hold on to his or her stock at all costs, and if anyone *had* to sell their shares, I requested they offer their shares to me first. My old school of thought was that no Raymond stock *should ever leave* the family. In my mind, the worst thing that could possibly happen would be to lose control of the company to an outsider.

Well, so much for old schools. I no longer cared. Suddenly I was *looking* for an outsider.

The first person I went to see after that fateful board meeting was my lawyer, Robert Hughes. He recommended I hire an outside company that could advise me as to my options. Even before doing that, I had a pretty good idea what they were. I could do nothing, I could sell my stock to the company, or I could force a sale of the company. The last option had a surreal ring to it. George Raymond Jr. engineering a sale of The Raymond Corporation! How did one sell one's life?

But selling the company was the only way for me to get what my stock was worth—*not* the $16 a share it had stayed at for so long but at a more realistic valuation. Now I thereby had to do what was best for my family, the other shareholders, and myself.

Acting on the advice of my attorney, I called a company in Cleveland, Ohio, that specialized in valuing companies the size of Raymond. Two men arrived who set about determining what the company might sell for. I had done my own figuring, based on Lou Durland's good-as-gold formula; now the gentlemen from Cleveland and I were not only in the same ballpark, we were all but hugging the same base. We concurred that the stock of The Raymond Corporation was greatly undervalued, and should be going for considerably more, anywhere between $25 and $30 a share.

Armed with the Columbus report, I prepared a slide presentation, which I then took to the board meeting that immediately followed the annual meeting on the first weekend in May, 1996. As a member of the board, I exercised the prerogative to call for an executive session of the board, which meant that only directors—no Raymond officers (except for Ross)—could attend.

Almost two months had passed since Ross Colquhoun had killed the nomination of Gail Webster for board membership. I knew that the board, especially Ross, would have liked nothing better than for me to stay in Florida, playing golf with Robin and leaving them to their own devices. Unfortunately for the directors and their chairman, I couldn't do that. My makeup, toughened on the playing fields of Greene High, had brought me back to my old hometown to do battle.

I displayed, verbatim, the statements I had written in my room in the Breakers. Then, using carefully prepared slides as talking points, I made a presentation to the board. My thrust was direct: I intended to sell the company.

When I had finished my talk, I said, "Today is Saturday. Day after tomorrow, on May 5, 1996, I'm filing a 13D with the Securities and Exchange Commission." A 13D is the document the SEC requires when any large stockholder of a publicly held company changes his investment objective and he must immediately make that fact known to the world. By Monday everyone on Wall Street would know that George G. Raymond, Jr. had just put The Raymond Corporation in play to be sold.

I could feel the resentment in the air, but the days when that would have bothered me were long gone. The directors tried talking me into changing my mind, or at least waiting, but I turned a deaf ear. I was determined to do what was best for myself, my family, and the shareholders.

To my distress, I learned that the 22 percent of the Raymond stock I personally owned would not be enough to control the sale of the company without outside help. I knew that Ross had been trying to swing a deal, using the company as a major bargaining chip, that would line his pockets at my expense. In a letter I wrote to him in November, I accused him of "shopping my shares" without consulting me.

At one point it looked as if Ross might be able to structure a deal that would put him and his board in control of a multinational, multibillion-dollar conglomerate. Needing money to finance the operation, he had Lehman Brothers issue $60 million in convertible debentures.

The deal fell through, however—shades of Jim Hardy—when Ross learned that his potential partners had a shaky financial base. The upshot was that Raymond suddenly had $60 million of new debt on its hands, thanks to Colquhoun's self-serving and ill-timed move.

I was greatly disturbed by this debt, and in the same letter I wrote to him in November, I said:

> As you know, I am also concerned to discover that management has not developed any proposal for how it intends to handle the convertible debenture, which is redeemable at a premium commencing on December 15, 1996. You have indicated you believe, as I do, that the present market price undervalues Raymond Shares. I cannot understand then why a redemption is not a priority rather than to permit a subsequent conversion at or about $18 per share. Certainly I have the clear impression that neither you nor the rest of the Board would believe it prudent to sell a new issue of shares at or about $18. Why then would we permit a conversion at this price when we have the cash for a redemption? I would like this issue promptly addressed as it comes up soon and affects the Company's valuation.

How Ross actually intended to pay off the debt, I wasn't sure, but I feared it would be in stock—that is, in new shares, which would water down the value of all existing shares, and hurt Raymond's current stockholders. I was beginning to see the man, whom I had personally entrusted to run the company, as not acting in the best interest of the Raymond shareholders. I remembered the day I had driven with him, immediately after he became Raymond's chief executive, and he suggested I move my office to Binghamton, so company personnel wouldn't be confused as to where directives were coming from. Of all the things in my life I should have seen through, I should have seen through that. Oh, to be in that car again so I could say, "Sorry, Ross. I'm happy in my Greene office. I'm staying."

But I didn't say it, and now I was in a fight to the finish with this same man. If the truth be told, I wasn't sure I would win. Twenty-two percent was far from the number of shares needed to force the sale of the company and Ross had access to the company's far-reaching financial and legal resources at his disposal as chairman and CEO. I felt like Horatius at the bridge, watching the enemy draw nigh.

I had alluded to a saying earlier: "Power corrupts, and absolute power corrupts absolutely." Not all men, but sure as hell some.

As Robin and I were sitting around our Naples home one day in early 1997, pondering the situation we found ourselves in, the phone rang. I picked it up. It was a man who said his name was Robert Lietzow, but that was all I heard—really all I wanted to hear. I told him I wasn't interested. Thank you, and goodbye.

Robin asked me what the call was about. "Nothing," I replied. "Just some broker trying to sell me something."

Three minutes later the phone rang again, and this time Robin answered. She listened with great interest, told the person to please hold, then said to me: 'It's a Mr. Lietzow from Metropolitan Capital in New York. He says he's not trying to sell you anything. He'd like to help you sell the company."

Puzzled, I took the phone, apologizing for cutting him short. Mr. Lietzow said he was an investment advisor, then repeated what he had just said to Robin. Because I was both a board member and a major stockholder in the company, I said to Mr. Lietzow, I would have to refer him to my lawyer, Robert Hughes, because I was under the SEC 13D restriction. Lietzow, obviously pleased that I hadn't brushed him off a second time, said he would call Mr. Hughes, and two weeks later all parties and lawyers met in New York in the office of one Jeffrey Schwartz, also an investment manager.

Gail Webster, as my personal investment manager, was there with the Huntington Bank's lawyer, and Robert Hughes, my lawyer, was representing me. Lietzow was in the room as were Schwartz and his attorney, Joseph Mazzella, from the Boston firm of Lane Altman & Owens. Lietzow had called me in Naples to make contact, but it soon became clear that Schwartz was the chief player. He had recently bought 10 percent of The Raymond Corporation's stock for about $10 million, intending to force a sale of the company, believing, as I did, that the stock was very much undervalued. I saw him as an experienced entrepreneur. When he asked me if I would vote with him at two successive Raymond annual meetings, I agreed.

Battle lines were forming, and with Schwartz's backing I saw myself in a strong position. Together, we had the muscle to sell the company. Ross, still thinking "big picture" with Raymond as his power base, was opposed to the sale. With Ross fast approaching retirement age, his investment objectives were similar to mine, but he didn't see it that way. I often have wondered why he didn't join forces with his friend and business associate to successfully complete the sale of the company once the decision was made.

The board of directors met in Tucson in March of 1997. I had expected the usual group of directors and company officers, but I was amazed to see three strangers seated in chairs somewhat apart from the main table.

As I was walking in to take my place, Ross piped up: "You're excused, George."

"You can't excuse a director!" I snapped.

"If you don't leave we'll adjourn and hold a rump session in someone's room in the hotel," replied the in-house lawyer, Paul Sternburg.

I thought about it. I could kick and holler, take my place and watch the directors file out; or I could leave and let them go about their business. Neither my vote, nor any words I might say, would deter Ross Colquhoun from his agenda, whatever it was. Telling myself the only way to handle his dismissiveness was to walk quickly. I walked away from Ross and his feckless board.

I hadn't taken five steps from the meeting room when I heard the "click" of a lock behind me. For a long moment I stood there struggling with my emotions. They were locking me out, the founder's son, who had dedicated his life to the company. I kept asking myself, What do I do? What is the right thing to do? In my mind, I saw my father looking down at me, his eyes expressive. Were they telling me, "George, go back! Knock down that door, tell those sons-of-bitches where to get off!"? Or was his gaze saying, "You're doing the right thing. Ross Colquhoun isn't worth the spit you'd lose shouting"?

My father's image faded, but not before I understood the wisdom in his face. I looked back at the bolted door, then turned and kept walking.

It was at that meeting, I learned later, that the "strangers" in the room—Lehman Bros. executives and their lawyer—convinced the Raymond board that they couldn't win a proxy fight. In other words, shareholders—namely the major financial institutions such as Trust Company of the West, Pioneer, and Babson, which held 70 percent of Raymond's stock—would vote against the board, knowing that they would receive a much higher price than they'd paid.

Ross thought—until Lehman Bros. set him straight—that he controlled the financial institution vote. He had recently taken top executives from all three institutions to Alaska for a week of trout and salmon fishing. No way would they go against the wishes of the chairman of The Raymond Corporation—unless someone were to promise them a little profit, a nice return on their original investment. With the sale of the company, they would cash in.

There was another reason why these financial institutions were ready to vote against Ross. Before the company could be sold, the debentures he had floated to finance his multi-billion-dollar deal in 1994 would have to be paid down in full. Holders of these bonds could redeem them for cash or Raymond stock, and virtually everyone would take stock, on the theory and belief that its value was going up. Smart move, but the adding of $60 million of *new* stock to the total number of outstanding shares diluted the value of those shares already owned by stockholders. The financial institutions weren't pleased. Whatever the company would sell for, the debt payoff figured to cut their take by one-third. And mine. And the take of every single Raymond shareholder!

For a number of reasons, Raymond stockholders were generally in an angry mood in 1996 and 1997. The board, under the command of Ross Colquhoun, would not only *lose* a proxy fight; it would be a massacre.

Once Lehman finished its presentation, Ross and the board had no choice; they voted, if begrudgingly, to sell the company. For the next several weeks, Lehman Bros. looked for a buyer, and at a subsequent meeting the board voted to give themselves substantial bonuses for their "work" in bringing about the sale. I had done more toward that end than all of them put together and didn't get a dime. I wasn't even reimbursed for my expenses, now well over half a million dollars.

I saw Ross on the last evening of the Tucson meeting, as he, his board members and their wives were having cocktails in the lobby. "George," he said, as if nothing had happened, as if his duplicitous actions of the past two years were so much water under the bridge, "stay and have dinner with us."

I had nothing planned, nowhere special to go. "Thank you," I said. "I have another engagement."

At 6 P.M. on Sunday, June 15, 1997, all Raymond directors assembled in the lobby of the Waldorf in New York City before going to the law firm of Simpson Thacher & Bartlett, where the "closing" would take place. We had a buyer. Actually six companies wanted to buy Raymond. Ross issued an order. We would go on foot, as a unit. It was only a couple of blocks. Forward, march!

Well, the couple of blocks turned out to be closer to fifteen! I was walking with a cane, because of recent hip-replacement surgery. The platoon of Raymond stalwarts passed me and Robert Hughes quickly by. The impression I got was that they wanted to leave us in the dust; maybe we might get lost along the way! We arrived ten minutes after everyone else—to the announcement that the board wasn't allowing Bob into the law firm's main conference room. I wanted to argue the point, fed up with Ross and his power plays, but Bob, never one to take his eye off the ball, reminded me what our objectives were. So I went in alone.

Of the six interested companies, only BT Enterprises, a Swedish firm, offered its bid with the required proof that it could meet the price, and when the last document was signed later that evening, BT became Raymond's parent company, agreeing to pay shareholders $33 a share for their stock, for a grand total of $353 million.

I was pleased by BT's price but struck, at the same time, by feelings of sadness and loss. BT representatives were downstairs, planning to come up and meet the Raymond team. While we waited several board members walked up to me to shake hands, as if to say, "It's over now. No hard feelings." But I didn't offer my hand in return. I stood there, isolated. Ross came up, all smiles. If he had fought the sale, he sure liked the sound of the jingle in his pockets: $33 a share! Newly divorced, he would retire in splendor with the woman he had recently married, his secretary for many years.

I gave Ross a long, last look, ignored his offered hand, and walked out.

Bob Hughes and I went to the Oyster Bar in the Plaza, had a good drink and a fine dinner. We talked quietly, and I began to feel better, part of the human race again. The company was gone, but the feeling of isolation I had felt so keenly was fading. I thought of the years that still lay ahead, the challenge of starting a new business. A great and true friend was sitting across from me, and Robin was waiting for me at home.

The next day, after breakfast, Bob and I went to pay Jeffrey Schwartz a visit. In his office, we all shook hands, embraced, congratulated each other, thanked each other. It kept going on and on. If ever four grown men formed a Mutual Admiration Society, Jeffrey Schwartz, Robert Lietzow, Bob Hughes, and George Raymond Jr. chartered one that morning. And I shared with them again a fact that I alone had known first-hand: That 78 years earlier my father had bought a company—for nothing down and $6,000 in future profits.

13

Measure
of the Man

I n February, 1995, not long after the meeting at which Ross
Colquhoun blocked Gail Webster from joining the Raymond
board, I became disabled for a time. We'd been in Palm Beach to
see Robin's daughter, Amy, ride in a competition, and to stay
with her other daughter, Laurie. Amy invited us to follow her out to
the barn to see her horses, new truck and horse trailer. She'd warned
that it was a good hike, and, after a bit I wondered if I could make it
to the barn. Once we were there, I started to take some pictures, but
had trouble with the camera because my hands were trembling. Not
long after that, as I was driving away, the car suddenly veered to the
right, almost hitting a mailbox. When I almost hit the next one,
Robin asked loudly "Are you alright?"

Well, I pulled myself together, or so I thought, and focusing all my
energy and attention drove back to Naples at a steady sixty miles an
hour. But when we stopped at a carry-out on Alligator Alley, I spilled
two cups of coffee. Though I was able to hide one spill from Robin,
she saw the other one and I had to admit to her that I didn't feel very
well, but I insisted on driving all the way. When we got home, Annie
Stackhouse, Robin's Yoga-teaching friend who was visiting at the
time, suspected something was wrong and phoned her mother who
was a nurse, and gave this unthinkable diagnosis: "It sounds like a

stroke." I thought strokes happened to other men, not to Raymonds.

I took a shower, but by then it was obvious to Robin I was ill and she insisted on driving me to the emergency room. By the time we got there, I was slurring words and couldn't sign my name; that scared me, and when the hospital staff saw I was having trouble they started doing things in a hurry! My doctor, George Ferguson, asked me several questions, including the names of the recent Presidents in reverse order; I got stuck on Nixon! And the doctor said "Mr. Raymond, you've already had a stroke. This is serious business, and the next three days will be critical. I have to tell you that one out of three patients in this condition doesn't make it." Well, *that* got my attention, and I realized I'd better start cooperating fast.

I was in the hospital for thirteen days while they tried to get the right mix of medications. The worst thing physically was that I couldn't straighten my right hand, and had some speech difficulties. But I began to do the exercises they prescribed, and Annie worked with me on special exercises based on her Yoga background. (I still do a number of them.)

That summer, in Nantucket, where we went to recuperate, I had a terrible case of shingles, but mostly I just rested. I had another setback when I had a hip replacement operation, which meant more drugs and physical therapy. By then I was ready to admit that if I didn't change my life style, my days were numbered. So I watched my diet, gave up alcohol, and found I had the strength to face the problems in my life—starting with the sale of The Raymond Corporation, but not ending there. No indeed; there was the Raymond Foundation to see to.

The Raymond Foundation, like the Company, went back before my era to my father's. He and I had funded it with the grand sum of $100, if memory serves, for the essentially civic purpose of helping the town of Greene with a variety of small projects. When Dad died, he left the Foundation $1 million in Raymond Corporation stock, which helped him estate-tax-wise, and made it possible for the Foundation to make larger and more frequent grants. My parents, my wife Cynnie and I were the first trustees, and later I added towns-people in order to make the Foundation more representative of the community. There was a teacher, a doctor, and one non-family person from The Raymond Corporation. Years later, when they became adults, we added my three children as trustees.

In 1985, the year before I stepped down as CEO, the local news-paper asked me to write something about the obligation of a wealthy person or company to help others. In my article, I touched on the history and purpose of the Foundation.

> Six members of the Greene community or employees of the Raymond Corporation and four members of the Raymond family were asked to serve three-year terms as trustees. In this way, we were able to share our wealth with the community and those in need, while making sure that the charitable decision-making continued to be done at a very high level. The foundation also ensures a steady flow of funding even in the lean years, and allows members of the community and employees of our company to join in making the decisions of where the money should go.
>
> The foundation trustees established objectives and policies to guide the Use of Funds committee in their evaluation of fund requests. For example, the foundation is very interested in assisting in "start-up" situations. They do not fund repetitively yearly operating funds.
>
> The Raymond family has limited the trustees' power with specific directions. The trustees are free in very broad parameters, to manage the foundation funds. Through the foundation, we are able to provide money from our private funds and from our corporation, for education cultural, health and religious purposes. Through the foundation, we are able to identify with and assist in, the solution of community problems; encourage group action to serve the needs of the community not currently being met; and further The Raymond Corporation's philosophy that people function best in a free society within an organization with high ethical standards and with full consideration for the individual.

The Foundation continued in its middle-of-the-road manner until 1997, when the company was sold and its stock jumped to $33 a share. Then the stock held by the Foundation, which had paid few dividends in recent history, suddenly soared in value. As far as the Foundation was concerned, BT Enterprises was the goose that laid a golden egg! The Foundation found close to $5.5 million in its till— no longer in shares, but in hard cash. If wisely invested, this money would ensure the financial viability of the Foundation indefinitely.

That same year, 1997, two important things happened—one of them purely redemptive, and the other highly creative, although it would lead inexorably to one of the most destructive episodes in my life.

The redeeming event occurred when Robin and I discovered and then joined our new church, Unity of Naples. Robin first saw this sanctuary nestled among trees, and she was reminded of another church in a quiet Florida wood, the church where we had held the funeral service for her son, Billy, who'd died suddenly fourteen years earlier. She mourned deeply, and mourns still, the loss of the beautiful young man she so deeply loved; now, through Unity of Naples they are close once again. Beyond that, both Robin and I find our lives enriched by the inspiration of two ministers, Jack Kern and Art Holt, who teach their flock to follow the path "From Success to Significance." Unity of Naples shows us the way to find new fullness and peace.

As for the cataclysm, it arose out of the new enterprise I founded in 1997, Sankaty Capital Management, L.L.C. Using my proceeds from the buyout, I started my own investment firm in Naples with my lawyer and old friend, Robert Hughes. The man who set up the firm was the former Securities and Exchange Commission counsel, Joseph Mazzella (who remains Sankaty's attorney). Our firm, named after the 185-year-old Sankaty lighthouse on Nantucket, invests and manages money for individual clients and private charitable organizations... like the Raymond Foundation—thus the deluge.

Once the dust of the sale to BT had settled, and Sankaty Capital Management was up and running, I had planned to present myself and my new firm to the Foundation. At this point in its history, my daughter Jean and son Steve were inactive trustees while Pete, the executive director of the Foundation who lived in Greene, did the lion's share of the work. He had indicated to me, in August of that year, that the door was wide open to Sankaty Capital Management. "You're the only living founder, Dad," he told me. "However you want to manage the funds is all right with me."

I was pleased by Pete's comment, and the sentiment behind it, and shortly afterward I requested the meeting with the Foundation board. I wanted to formally introduce my partner and offer Sankaty's services to the Foundation as its investment arm. I couldn't think of a single reason why we wouldn't succeed in our bid. Considering my background with Raymond and the history of the Foundation, originated by my father and me thirty-five years earlier, it seemed a natural.

My second son, Steve, who for the past ten years had operated a Raymond dealership in California, decided he would attend that meeting, to be held at Baron's Inn in Greene in December 1997. At Steve's suggestion, the family members had decided to meet at Pete's house before moving on to the scheduled meeting of the full board at 10 A.M.

Bob Hughes, Joseph Mazzella and I arrived at 8:00. Steve, Jean and the chairman of the Foundation's trustees, Greene businessman Jim Barton, were also there. Steve started off the informal gathering with a series of blunt, fast-paced statements and accusations directed at Joe Mazzella, who had spent five years as counsel of the SEC, Robert Hughes, and me. What Steve said was this: Sankaty Capital is a start-up company, it has no track record, he didn't know Mr. Hughes personally or Mr. Mazzella at all; in short, he didn't feel comfortable handing over five and a half million dollars to our Naples-based firm. I felt Steve's comments to be inappropriate and disrespectful; furthermore I was deeply hurt by his lack of faith in me. Then Jean, who had no background in business or investments, spoke up. "Dad," she said, "this just doesn't smell good to me either."

Were these my children speaking? What did they think I was going to do, run off to Rio with the Foundation's funds?

About 9:30 we broke up and drove to Baron's for the board meeting, where Steve followed his first act with an equally harsh second, by denigrating me, Bob and Joe in front of the full board, most of whom I had asked to be a trustee of the Raymond Foundation. Steve was basically a kind, even-tempered guy, and for the life of me I couldn't figure out what was agitating him.

I suddenly realized it was only my children who were asking the questions. The other board members remained silent, as my own children relentlessly challenged our proposal. Clearly Steve and the other board members did not listen of a word of our presentation, nor to the materials Joe Mazzella had prepared detailing the concept of Sankaty Capital Management and the fact that we had hired five of the best fund managers on Wall Street to manage Sankaty funds.

After the meeting we all had lunch in Baron's dining room. The Foundation was leaning toward the New York investment firm of Bessemer. I put on a game face, having learned years ago that salesmen have to take a lot of abuse, then grin and bear it. I could hardly believe what had happened. I had just finished battling Ross Colquhoun for two years, and now I was battling my children! I couldn't wait to leave. It was one of the lowest points of my life.

I returned to Naples, feeling betrayed and emotionally drained. A day or two later Pete called and said, "Dad, we've decided to

limit our investment in Sankaty to $250,000 [the minimum portfo-
lio the firm would handle]—as a trial run." I told him to forget it.
Sankaty Capital Management wasn't looking for a handout. Thanks,
but no thanks. After all, the Raymond Foundation was now worth
$5.5 million.

I stewed for the rest of the week. Robin was deeply dismayed by
the turn of events in Greene, specifically the rejection of me by my
children, and she saw the emotional pain that I was going through. So
soon after my struggles with Ross, I didn't need another major battle.
Finally I called Pete and leveled with him, telling him how upset I
was. To my surprise, he seemed surprised to hear it. Perhaps my game
face in Baron's had worked, but how could he think, deep down, I
wasn't injured?

Pete wrote to Robin shortly after Christmas 1997, to explain his
position and apparently to gain some insight into why I was so angry.
Entitled "I'm Confused," his e-mail said, in part:

> Dad contacted me indicating that his new business wanted to take the
> responsibility for the Foundation's investments, and he would like to
> make a presentation to the Trustees. Based on preliminary information,
> the Trustees felt that the investment strategies and techniques employed
> by Sankaty were inappropriate for the Foundation. However, since this
> involved Dad, the Trustees felt obligated to listen to the presentation....
>
> Sankaty made the presentation, the Trustees met to review that data, and
> agreed, because Dad was involved, to invest the minimum $250,000.
> The remaining assets of the Foundation (all 5 million of it) would be
> invested with Bessemer. When I communicated the decision to Dad, he
> expressed extreme disappointment....The logic seems to be, "If you are
> not for me, you must be against me." I do not view it this way. The
> Foundation was faced with a business decision. The Trustees, using their
> best judgment, and leaning as far as, in good conscience, they could
> toward Dad's program, made the decision. I do not understand how it
> has become such a personal issue.

Robin could hardly believe that my son couldn't see why I had taken the rejection so hard. In her reply to Pete, she wrote:

> Your letter had all the explanations—policies and objectives of the Trustees on how to invest the Foundation's monies. I am sure you have studied all the "angles" and have unanimously voted to go with Bessemer.
>
> Pete, I am here to tell you that a sword went through your father's heart when you called, in logical fashion, and delivered the news that you were putting the Foundation's money elsewhere.... Here he was, one of the original founders of the Foundation, trying to tell you how they [he and Bob Hughes] would expand the Foundation's assets, and he returned home feeling that the air was as hostile as if he was asking to have the funds put into his own bank account!
>
> God knows your Dad went to hell and back trying to sell the company. He, as the leader for 45 years, suffered indignities from Ross, his hand-picked CEO, and the board, that were worthy of lawsuits.... You know the fight that ensued, when everyone thought he was crazy to even think he could ask 25 dollars a share—and look what happened! He settled his family affairs by taking care of his family and his sister's family by making you all wealthy, and he has yet to hear a word of gratitude. And by the way, it was only through his efforts that the Foundation coffers got filled to overbrimming.
>
> I want to add one more thing about the "bill" which your father incurred when he sold the company. He paid all the expenses for *you* getting $33 a share! You call that *his* problem? Your father, being the good, trusting man that he is, paid [expenses] for the shares of you, Steve and Jean because he wanted to spare you the expense yourselves. Madeleine [his sister] paid her share. The Foundation stands out. Why should George pay that too?
>
> Your non-acceptance has been a bitter pill to swallow. You said the logic seems to be "if you are not for me, you must be against me." I think you might be absolutely right. A manly, parental nerve was cut. This has nothing to do with "anger," as you express it, but with pain and suffering.

Not long after the exchange of letters, Steve phoned me and said, "Dad, we have to resolve this. Marnie and I are flying down to see you."

Realizing I was still too upset to have a rational discussion, I told him they should hold off making the trip, but Steve argued that they had already bought plane tickets and had rearranged their work schedules in California. I said all right, but then phoned Steve back, telling him it just wasn't a good time for me. I was weary, feeling a bit unanchored, and he should cancel his flight. Thirty minutes later Marnie called Robin, saying, indignantly, that she and Steve had done a great deal of shifting and juggling of schedules, and it was unfair to put them off.

The bottom line was, they were *all* coming—Steve, Marnie, Pete, and Jean. Finally, in desperation, Robin called Dick Beckhard. I had never heard her voice so strained as when she said, "We really need your help."

What he said was, "Let them come. This could possibly be the last family meeting George will have with his kids. Let him have it, but make it blood family only—no Robin, no daughters-in-law, no lawyers. Just George and his children."

Following Dick's advice, Robin left the house the next morning at 8:00, and my kids arrived shortly afterward, minus Marnie. I was glad to see them, even though I wasn't sure what might be gained by the visit. Because they were here, however, I decided to make the most of it. The four of us talked for a while sitting around the pool—at least Steve and I talked. Nothing heavy or deep, and the confrontational tone was gone from his voice. He was more like the soft-spoken, even-tempered Steve I knew, and it made me wonder all over again what had bugged him in Greene. Pete and Jean, in keeping with their natures, hardly said a word.

After twenty minutes, the kids and I drove to my Sankaty office in Newgate Tower in Naples. I showed them around, pointing at the model of the Sankaty lighthouse in Nantucket on the foyer table. Then I suggested we do an "issues and concerns" as a way of bringing closure to the emotionally charged meeting in Greene. As I was setting up the flip-chart, however, I started feeling unsteady, unsure I could lead the discussion effectively. Perhaps I was more worn down by the recent events in my life than I realized. I sat down and asked Pete to take over.

I made the point, as we started in, that we should not deal with the future of the Foundation, but we did need closure on what had happened in Greene. The non-support of my children was, for me, the crowning blow of the past two painful and exhausting years. I had come to feel like an outsider in my own house.

We stayed at it through the entire morning, kicking around issues like the hostility at the Foundation meeting, the difference between a "family decision" and a "business decision," the lack of faith on the children's part in my new business and partnership. This last point we spent twenty minutes discussing, though not in a way that did any more than scratch the surface.

We limped along into the third hour. The subject of the sale of The Raymond Corporation came up, and Steve said he wasn't happy about it. I thought the comment interesting, considering how well they had all done financially. My father had given each of his grandchildren a large chunk of Raymond stock, and now they were free to do what they wanted for the rest of their lives.

"What's to be unhappy about?" I said. "You're set. All of you are!"

"Maybe in terms of money," Steve said, "but when you sold the company we just became an ordinary family."

We sat for a long moment, as if in mourning, as if someone dear to us had died, someone we'd watched grow from infancy. "We never wanted the company sold, Dad," Steve went on, emotion etched on his brow. "I mean, we're all upset. You pulled the rug from underneath us! How can we trust you?"

Maybe they couldn't. It was something we would all have to live with.

I remembered the day in grade school, so many years ago, when Mrs. Schmoll had called my father a "savior." I was happy that she thought of him so highly, but to me he was just an ordinary dad who worked hard, came home for dinner, and took me hunting and fishing on weekends. I never saw him put on airs, and I sure as hell never did either. But what Steve said struck a chord in me, nonetheless. With BT's purchase of Raymond, we'd lost an identity. We were all still Raymonds, and always would be, but the name across the back of our old company jackets could now just as well read SMITH or JONES. Something was gone. Perhaps my children felt it more strongly than I.

We went out for lunch, then came back to my office for another four hours of fruitless talk. I could only wish Dick Beckhard was with us to make sure we had established a process for our discussion. We each came to the table with different subjects and different priorities. We drifted for the rest of the afternoon and never resolved any issues. Steve had a plane to catch and time was starting to close in, so when we finished he and I went back to the house on Grand Bay Drive. Pete and Jean, in their own car, would be along shortly.

When Steve and I reached the house, Robin was there and greeted Steve warmly. She was sorry he couldn't stay. Did he have time for a cup of coffee?

He thanked her but said he was afraid he'd miss his plane.

"Well, how did it go?" Robin asked.

"At least I know I'm not an orphan!" he said, smiling.

We walked Steve out to his car and he drove off.

"What did he mean?" Robin asked

"Maybe he thought I was going to disown him."

Ten minutes later Pete and Jean arrived; they seemed detached, almost unfriendly. As brother and sister, they had always had emotions and thoughts in common. They were on the same wavelength. At no time was it more obvious than at that moment, when they came in and sat down. Robin asked the same question of Pete she had asked of Steve. How had the meeting gone with his father?

"I guess all right, but I don't know how I'll feel about it tomorrow."

There was a long silence. "Well, can I get you anything?" Robin said. "Jean, a cup of tea?"

"No, thank you."

We sat down in the living room. Robin tried her best to make Pete and Jean feel at home, to no avail; they wouldn't give or loosen up. We might all have been sitting in a bus terminal, strangers at that. Robin and I had a dinner date with friends, but she told me it was best if we canceled. She went to the phone and changed the date for tomorrow, which everyone heard her do.

Then, with a smile and open arms, she asked my children if they would like a drink. She then said, "Oh, good. Now we can all have dinner together."

As she was running through a couple of menu ideas, Pete interrupted. "Don't bother, Robin. We're tired. We won't be staying." It was only 7 P.M.

And just like that they got up and left.

For a few minutes afterward neither of us spoke. I sat on the sofa, trying to assimilate my feelings, ranging from disappointment to downright anger. Next thing I knew, Robin was sitting next to me. She took my hand. "You did everything you could," she said.

"I'm not sure I did."

"You did, George. No one wins them all." Her eyes were damp. "We have the rest of our lives, together. I love you!"

More than anything, it was what I had to hear. A rift between a man and his children is a deep wound and would take a long time to heal. The strength I felt from my wife would help me come to terms with all that had happened.

Looking back at those meetings, both at Pete's house and at Baron's, I see clearly now what I didn't see then, that the sale of the company had done irreparable damage to my family. I had sold The Raymond Corporation in part to protect my own and my family's stake, and in part out of financial necessity to prevent the need for tremendous immediate cash requirements to pay estate taxes upon my death. My family would have no source of cash except through the distress sale of the company. But in doing so I had toppled the "House of Raymond" that had stood, as a symbol of our family unity for seven decades. I no longer sat at the head of the table. As my children saw it, the sale of The Raymond Corporation was a betrayal of our family heritage.

Life goes on, and from time to time praise, or recognition, falls our way. I was happy when the town of Greene, New York, dedicated a new athletic field complex to me in the fall of 1999, for my part, via the Raymond Foundation, in bringing the project to fruition. I wasn't able to attend the ceremony, at which State Senator Thomas Libous was present, but I was duly represented by Pete.

When the good people of Greene had first heard I intended to sell the company, they were deeply concerned, and some no doubt thought I had turned my back on the community. I feared I would be *persona non grata* in my old hometown.

Well, I sold the company, but BT kept it going—same old name, same old location—and they're doing very well. Employment is strong. So I'm not the bad guy I thought I might become. I was deeply touched by the plaque that bears my name at the entrance to the athletic complex, and by Mayor John Bennett's words on a Certificate of Appreciation.

George has shared his time, talent, and treasure with the community in many ways. His contributions to the Greene Central School, Greene Fire Department and Emergency Squad, and to the Lions Club Park are only some of his numerous contributions, which have affected all residents of Greene, past, present and future.

That same fall I received another tribute, this one from Alfred University, which honored me at a luncheon at Chicago's Drake Hotel. Twenty-six business students and five faculty members were in Chicago for the annual conference of the Family Firm Institute, and they attended the luncheon. Five years earlier Alfred had taken a wish of mine to heart and had established the Center for Family Business and Entrepreneurial Leadership in their Business College, and in 1998 Robin and I gave $2 million to endow a faculty chair in family business.

When the luncheon ended, I spoke a few words to the assembled people—the Alfred group and 175 guests from the FFI convention. I told them how proud I was to be a life trustee of Alfred University, an honor granted me in 1993, and how excited I was knowing that the Center was among the leaders, here and abroad, in providing education and research opportunities in family business. It was a vision I had had for a long time, and it was vastly rewarding for me to see it come true.

And how it has come true! In the summer of 2000, we established the George G. and Robin Raymond Family Business Institute at Alfred, a teaching institution that intends to become the premiere leadership organization for family businesses nationally and internationally. Its goals: to address a niche family business market through the provision of start-up, organizational, financial and networking services; to lead family businesses to operational and financial success; to promote all aspects of family business growth and development through education, training and research initiatives and services; to stimulate family business leadership; and to contribute significantly to

ongoing academic and entrepreneurial conversations regarding family business.

To mark the founding, newly retired president of Alfred University,
Edward G. Coll, Jr. issued a statement on "George Raymond's Family
Business Legacy at Alfred University." It reads in part:

> Beginning in the early 1980s George Raymond, Chairman of the
> Alfred University Board of Trustees, focused the University's attention
> on the opportunity to create a program that would serve the special
> needs of family businesses. Recognizing the importance of family busi-
> nesses and entrepreneurial ventures in creating this country's prosperity,
> the administration and Board of Trustees at Alfred University in 1994
> created the Center for Family Business and Entrepreneurial Leadership.
> Like other entrepreneurial ventures, this entailed some risk in the highly
> competitive market of higher education, but the risk has paid off for the
> University. The program has allowed us to distinguish our College of
> Business from the host of other business schools available to students
> today. The Center for Family Business and Entrepreneurial Leadership
> has grown to become one of the country's preeminent educational and
> research facilities focusing on family business and entrepreneurship.
>
> George Raymond and his wife Robin created the Raymond Chair in
> the Family Business with a gift of $2 million. The trustees of Alfred
> University have followed George's example and have lent their finan-
> cial support to the project as well. A $1 million gift from former
> AU trustee Jon Tabor and his wife, Mary, funds the Tabor Chair in
> Family Business. The University also has an endowed professorship
> in entrepreneurship—the William T. Tredennick Professor of Entre-
> preneurship—held by Dr. Robert Hutter. A gift from the estate of the
> late Mr. Tredenncik, who served Alfred University as a trustee for
> nearly forty years, will allow us to advance that professorship to a third
> endowed chair, which will be termed the William T. Tredennick Chair
> in Entrepreneurship. Although other universities are interested in
> family business issues, none can boast three endowed professorships.

President Coll's statement goes on to list some of the organizations
and foundations that are participating in the funding of the Center.
Among them are the Emerson Foundation with a gift of $500,000; a

gift of $250,000 from the Galanis family; a gift of $100,000 from Erick and Marianne Laine and the Cutco Foundation; two grants totaling $100,000 from the Kauffman and Coleman Foundations.

Ed Coll concluded by saying—and I write his comment here with due modesty, but with no small pride—"Today, George Raymond is working to extend the influence of Alfred University's Center even further. He created the Raymond Family Business Institute at Alfred. The Institute promotes the growth and development of family business through education, training and research. This venture promises to expand Alfred University's reach, and the reach of George Raymond's dreams, to worldwide audiences."

But one can't live on praise alone. It is the icing on the cake of a job well done and shouldn't make us think we've arrived, even that we're successful. Until the good Lord says, "That's it. Now you may rest," I intend to go out and earn my daily bread.

I do not know the meaning of "retire." My joy is, and always has been, the job. I go to my office at Sankaty Capital Management each day with the same enthusiasm I had as a young man, when I first began working for my father.

If work brings rewards, I've certainly had a share, but rewards cannot be a goal. Make them a goal, they are forever elusive. The joy is in the doing. I would rather come home with scraped knuckles than sit all day in luxury. The scars make me know I'm alive, that I've been out there fighting the good fight.

Though no one could have seen it when my parents arrived in Greene and my father sat behind his desk at Lyon Iron Works for the first time, I was to be part of a truly American story of enterprise and family, of blows suffered and goals attained. As I grow older, a sense of gratitude overrides all, perhaps to a higher power than I ever really knew, for the opportunity I had and for the life I was given.

Acknowledgments

I am deeply grateful to several people who helped me with this book in several ways—through their expressed encouragement, their active help with particular tasks, their tacit support, their particular skills.

Ten years ago I had a dream about writing my autobiography. I confided this to my late friend, colleague and brother, Dick Beckhard, whose opinion I valued, and who was the author of several successful books himself. I expected him to laugh at the notion, because I am simply not a writer, but to my astonishment he said very sincerely, "Yes, that's a good idea."

The idea lay dormant for six years until Dick and his wife, Sandra Barty, invited me and my wife, Robin, to join them on their annual sailing vacation in the British Virgin Islands. When Sandy started asking me questions about my past, the thoughts, memories and feelings suddenly started tumbling out. Over the next ten days I talked constantly and she filled several legal pads with my rambling story. Perhaps it was the open sea or the fact that I had just sold my business that hastened and increased the flow of the words, which she recorded. I am indebted to Sandy for actually beginning the process of unwinding the story of my life.

Later, John Greenya, an experienced hand at composing memoirs, took Sandy's raw notes, augmented them with material from his many taped conversations with Robin and me, and wrote a working draft.

It is to Anthony Robinson that I express special appreciation, for deepening and expanding the working draft—for helping me put my life into words with nuance and new depth, and new anecdotes of his own recollection. Tony knows me and my family intimately, in addition he knew the dynamics of the Raymond Corporation, and finally he is an accomplished novelist in his own right. It was with an artist's sensitivity and a novelist's skill that he fleshed out my story.

When it came time to gather illustrations, Mrs. Mildred Pixley searched the archives in the Moone Memorial Library in Greene, New York, and worked most diligently—the epitome of the good neighbor.

Also, I am deeply grateful to Philip Kopper, the publisher and chief editorial officer of Posterity Press, for believing in this book and guiding it with a skilled and dedicated hand from start to finish.

Finally, I gratefully acknowledge this book's debt to Robin. She has been an active participant in every stage of the process, whether in making contributions to the original material, in refreshing my memory, or in reading proofs with her eagle eye. I thank her especially for her artistic intuition about style and tone, and her passionate commitment to the quality of the book.

Photo Credits:

Most of the photographs come from the author's personal collection. These include: the inset on page 101; all on pages 102-103, 104-105, 106-107, 108-109; top and lower right 112, bottom 113, 114-115 and 116-117.

Several portraits were taken by Robin Raymond, formerly Robin Ylvisaker. These include the frontispiece, dust jacket author's portrait, back dust jacket picture, lower left and top 113.

The photographs on pages 110-111 and the front cover subject, found in company archives, are published through the courtesy of The Raymond Corporation.

The historical photograph of the Lyon Iron Works, pages 100-101, appears through the courtesy of the Moore Memorial Library, Greene, New York.

Index

Note: page references in *italic* type refer to illustrations

All in the Family… Business was designed by Gerard A. Valerio of Bookmark Studio in Annapolis, Maryland.

Composed in Bembo and Clarendon by Janette Lockhart Nield.

Printed on 70# Finch Opaque Vellum by Schneidereith & Sons Printing, Baltimore, Maryland.